YOUR PET BIRD

Also by Michele Lowell

Your Purebred Puppy:
A Buyer's Guide

YOUR PET BIRD

A Buyer's Guide

MICHELE LOWELL

HENRY HOLT AND COMPANY

NEW YORK

Henry Holt and Company, Inc.
Publishers since 1866
115 West 18th Street
New York, New York 10011

Henry Holt® is a registered
trademark of Henry Holt and Company, Inc.

ISBN 0-8050-2325-9

DESIGNED BY LUCY ALBANESE

Printed in the United States of America

Photo credits appear on page 207.

To Scooter, our feisty blue-spangled budgie, who hurls her toys from her playground, peers curiously at the guinea pigs, and refuses to say anything except fweep. *And to Sprite, our flirtatious green-pied budgie: may he one day figure out that his little plastic bird friend will never return his hopeful advances.*

Contents

Talking parrots • Large or small? • Experience level required • The best birds for your children • Feathers, tails, and colors • Active or calm • Expensive and inexpensive birds

Acknowledgments

Thanks to my family for their help in driving around, snapping photos, and bringing me ginger ale when I needed it! Randy, you're only eight years old, but you were the biggest help of all by feeding the birds for me when I was busy. Thanks to Jane Gelfman, whose sad-funny-true bird stories perfectly illustrated what can happen when well-meaning people get stuck with the wrong bird; and to Alison Juram, who was patient and flexible through delays. And a special "birdie" thanks to Daunice Parker, Marion J. Sparzak, Diana Holloway, Brenda and K. P. Daigle of The Pampered Ones, and R. Gary for patiently answering all my questions and sending so many photos so promptly.

INTRODUCTION

Barbara Bernier wants to buy a pet bird for her family. A bird will chirp pleasantly and keep her amused while she works around the house. A bird will teach her kids valuable lessons in responsibility. A bird will perch prettily on a swing and play happily with toys. Canaries and parakeets are the obvious choices, she decides . . . but wait. Look at this pet shop ad: "Conures: Perky Parrots Make Perfect Pets!"

Parrots? Barbara is intrigued. Imagine owning an exotic parrot who would perch on her shoulder and entertain her guests with clever, witty phrases! Soon she is the proud owner of a lovely three-year-old nanday conure imported from South America.

The weeks go by. Paco climbs incessantly across the bars of his cage. He screeches so that nobody can hear the television. He shreds his wooden swing into ribbons. The only word he utters is a horrible obscenity in front of the minister. The only shoulder perching he does is accompanied by sharp nips at the closest human appendage. And the only lesson he has taught the kids is that conures nip very hard.

Soon his cage is moved from the family room to the spare bedroom. Then this ad appears in the paper: "Lovely Conure for Sale: Cheap!"

Where did the Berniers go wrong?

If you're in the market for a good-tempered, healthy pet bird for your family, you're holding the definitive step-by-step guide to finding one. *Your Pet Bird: A Buyer's Guide* will lead you through all the necessary steps to acquiring a nice bird: deciding whether a bird is the right pet for your family, choosing the right species, locating a reputable source for your species of choice, and selecting the best individual to join your family.

In our increasingly crowded society, prospective pet owners are turning more frequently to pets other than the traditional dogs and cats. Cats recently surpassed dogs as the number one pet in American households, and birds are closing in fast. But there is a staggering variety of birds out there—many more than the average person is aware of. Canaries and parakeets are not your only choices. Have you considered a Gouldian finch, an eclectus parrot, a rose-breasted cockatoo, a maroon-bellied conure, a chattering lory, a severe macaw, a white-capped pionus, a Pekin robin, a Senegal parrot?

This variety of available species means that you need plenty of honest, practical information if you are to choose wisely. But information that focuses on pet temperament and pet behavior is very difficult to find. Instead, most books describe the precise color of wing and tail coverts, the proper nest and preferred nesting grasses, special conditioning foods, how many eggs the female will lay, and how long she will incubate them. This is necessary information for breeders, but not for novices who simply want a pet.

Your Pet Bird: A Buyer's Guide is the book that pet owners have been waiting for. This is not a scientific book on ornithology nor is it an encyclopedia of bird species. It doesn't pretend to offer advice on breeding birds, nor on building and maintaining outdoor aviaries. Instead it is the first guide written especially for prospective bird owners who want to choose the right pet for their family.

So if you're a prospective bird owner and you have little or no knowledge of birds, take heart. You have one thing in common with experienced bird owners: the desire to share your home with a lovely winged creature. All you need now is honest and practical information. It is for you that this book was written, although experienced owners will also find comprehensive and clear behavioral information on the most popular pet birds in America.

Step One

DECIDING TO
GET A BIRD

1

SHOULD YOU GET A BIRD?

So, you think you want a pet bird?

Let's think about your decision some more. Let's talk about what it will mean to you, to your family, and to your present lifestyle. Let's be very sure you're making the right decision, because there's much more involved in owning a pet bird than you might have thought.

There's *money*.

Your purchase price may run from ten dollars for a parakeet to two thousand dollars for a rose-breasted cockatoo. This vast difference in price doesn't mean that a rose-breasted cockatoo is a better bird than a parakeet. Bird prices are determined by the popularity or rarity of a species, how readily the species breeds in captivity, how many eggs the species lays, and/or how easily the species can be imported.

In other words, supply and demand. So just because you're paying two hundred times more for a cockatoo than what you'd pay for a parakeet, you're not getting a bird *worth* two hundred times more. Pets are never really worth *money*—their worth is best expressed by how well they fit into your family and by how much you enjoy them. The ten dollar parakeet might be wonderful for you, while the two thousand dollar cockatoo might be a disaster. Or vice versa.

No species is perfect. All birds have good points and bad points. All birds are right for somebody and wrong for somebody else. That's the goal of this book: helping you find the bird who is right for *you*. And he doesn't have to cost two thousand dollars.

So if you have plenty of money, don't think anything more about how much one species costs or is "worth" compared to another. Think only in terms of finding the species that's best suited to your wants, needs, personality, and lifestyle—no matter how much or how little he costs.

But if you're like most of us, you probably live on some type of budget, so the initial cost of a bird will dictate, to some extent, the species you choose. But you'll be relieved to discover that there's a wide variety of birds available on the lower end of the scale. Unlike some other types of pets, there truly is a bird for every pocketbook.

Try not to cheat your budget by looking for bargains. For example, don't let your eyes light up at the sight of classified ads too good to be true: "Magnificent Rose-breasted Cockatoo, with Cage and all Supplies. Friendly, Healthy, Talks! Paid $2000. Will Sacrifice for $500 or Trade for Used Snowmobile."

Really now, how many people would "sacrifice" such a bird? Sure, some new owners have found nice birds through ads, but an expensive species is seldom offered for peanuts unless he has some behavioral problem. Especially suspect this to be true whenever a large parrot is offered cheap by a private party. Naturally, if you call the seller, he'll brush the problem aside or dance around it: "Oh, no, he's a great bird, he just needs more time and attention than we can give him."

Sure. You mean he bites, don't you?

Time and attention can work wonders in modifying and improving a bird's personality. But it has to be the right kind of time and attention, coupled with specific behavioral modification that is best determined and carried out by an experienced bird owner. It's very difficult for a novice to solve well-established behavioral problems.

Someday you might want to bring home a problem bird as a worthwhile rehabilitation project, but wait until you have more experience with birds. Right now, stick with normal birds that you can afford at normal prices.

≈　　≈　　≈

Though you've met the purchase price and placed your bird in his carrying case, the money outlay doesn't end. Buying birds is similar to buying fish: a goldfish costs a mere fifty cents, but the tank and supplies will run you another fifty dollars!

So you're strolling through the pet shop one day and the kids start begging: "Come on, Mom! Dad! What a great parakeet! Look, he's only ten bucks!" Ten dollars for a parakeet—fine, okay, cheap enough. But the cage costs fifty dollars and the swing and ladder and mirror and plastic bird companion and Olympic exercise rings and perch cleaner and net cost another thirty. Throw in ten dollars for the parakeet book and you've shelled out an even hundred. And you haven't yet made it to the bird food aisle.

Now—just for fun—stroll over to those heavy-duty wrought-iron parrot cages prominently displayed in the center aisle. Stop admiring them for a moment and note the prices: two hundred dollars, three hundred dollars. And for the large parrots who live in these cages, you'll need an additional playground, jungle gym, or T-stand because they won't remain tame (or quiet) if you try to keep them caged all the time. Playgrounds start at twenty dollars for a budgie-size model with a ladder and swing and go up to several hundred dollars for a macaw-size gym.

Speaking of the large parrots, you won't be buying just *one* set of toys. Powerful parrots don't carry those hooked beaks around just for show. They destroy their belongings with a cheerful regularity that is both amazing and dismaying. Replacement parrot toys will become a regular item in your family budget. So when you're buying a bird—even the tiniest finch or canary—the cost of cages and supplies is definitely a factor.

After you get your new bird home and settle him comfortably in his new cage with his first supply of new toys, you'll have to start filling his stomach with food.

For a small parakeet, you'll spend about ten dollars a month for a combination of pellet food, seeds, fruits and vegetables, and whole-wheat grains. (No, your bird will not thrive on seeds alone, no matter what your well-meaning grandmother says.) Naturally, as the size of the bird goes up, the food costs go up also.

You'll also have to buy mineral blocks, cuttlebones, and millet sprays. And you'll find yourself sneaking a box of "Birdie Biscuits" into your shopping cart every so often, so you better figure on an extra few dollars!

If you've chosen a medium or large parrot, the vet bills will start at thirty dollars for a yearly checkup. You can't let your guard down during the rest of the year either, because respiratory infections and annoying mites always seem to pop up at the most inconvenient times.

And if you've chosen a parrot, you'll probably be letting him out of his cage some of the time for taming and training, so you'll either have to learn how to clip his wings short or pay your vet or local bird store to do it for you. Occasionally, toenails and beaks may need to be trimmed as well. You may be able to handle the toenails, but the beak must be left to an expert.

If you take frequent business trips or if your family enjoys vacations, pet-sitting costs may be a factor, at five to fifteen dollars per day.

Money is indeed involved in owning a bird. *Time, attention,* and *household stability* are involved as well. Contrary to the casual remarks and encouragement of some pet store clerks, birds are not minimal-care pets. Consider if your line of reasoning goes something like this: "Our family wants a pet, but not a pet like a dog or a cat who needs lots of time and attention, maybe something simple like a bird. . . ." Well, boy are you in for a rude shock.

Birds are demanding—demanding of your time, demanding of your attention, and demanding of proper care. Some species are more demanding and harder to live with than a dog or a cat. Don't consider yourself a natural bird owner just because you've lived happily with dogs and cats. Birds are not feathered dogs or winged cats. Birds look at the world differently than do other pets, and they react differently to sights, sounds, and situations.

Also, birds are more susceptible to the slightest neglect. Your beagle would be hungry if she missed a meal, but she wouldn't become ill. Your finch, however, might die. Your tomcat would be cold if you left the window open on his favorite sleeping perch in the winter, but your canary might die. So if you're thinking about a bird because your busy lifestyle doesn't allow enough time and attention for a dog or cat, or if you thought that a bird would be the logical "next step down" in care requirements, it's simply not true.

Birds are not easier to care for than other pets. They cannot be forgotten. They are rigid and fussy about a clean cage, proper diet, consistent attention, and a predictable schedule. Birds require time and effort for feeding, for cleaning and washing their cage, for clipping their wings and toenails, for changing their bathwater, for talking and whistling to them, for checking their health, for nursing them when they aren't feeling well, and for taking them to the vet when necessary.

How much time does a bird need? The first requirement is that it be daily time, without fail. Pellets, seeds, fruits, vegetables, and water must be replaced daily, or your bird will not touch his food. You must examine his health daily. Birds are stoic, reluctant to show signs of weakness, so one missed day in detecting an illness might mean their life.

The daily time required varies by species. For a canary or parakeet, perhaps five or ten minutes of dedicated attention every morning and evening, with an additional fifteen minutes set aside each week for thorough cage cleaning, are sufficient. For a parrot or other large bird, the time shoots up to at least a half-hour and sometimes several hours every morning and evening. Parrots require more interaction—cuddling, petting, playtime, and/or training sessions for talking and doing tricks. Later in this book I talk extensively about the special socialization needs of parrots.

You must also set aside time for exercise. If your vision of a pet bird has him sitting quietly on a perch twenty-four hours a day, you must be thinking of a plastic toy. Birds are busy creatures. In the wild they flit from branch to branch, soar across meadows, hop through the grass in search of seeds and bugs, build nests, and groom each other. How often do you see a wild bird sitting still for very long?

Why, then, do people believe that pet birds don't need exercise? Maybe it's because pet birds are domesticated? Dogs are domesticated too, yet we acknowledge that dogs require time and space for running, jumping, and playing. Perhaps we forget about birds because they seem so small and insignificant. It's too easy to look upon them as beautiful ornaments and lock them up in a tiny cage, where the most exercise they get is hopping one perch down to the food dish.

In such an unnatural environment your bird may survive for a few years, but if surviving is all you had in mind for a pet, you should not get a pet. As responsible pet owners, our job is to provide a comfortable home and world for our pet, not a minimal shelter. That means exercise. Canaries, finches, and some small parrots can get enough exercise in a roomy cage, but most parrots need daily playtime on a freestanding perch, playground, or jungle gym. They require supervision during this playtime, so you must add more time required for ownership of parrots.

In determining whether you have the time available to care for a bird, you must consider not only the amount of time but also the regularity. Birds are not as flexible as dogs or cats; they prefer routines that are reliable and predictable. At approximately the same time each day, some member of your family should be available for feeding, cleaning, and/or socializing.

Birds react badly to change and instability. If your lifestyle is erratic, if people are running in and out of the house all day, if some nights you go to bed at nine and other nights the bright lights and loud music stay on until midnight, a bird is probably not a good pet for you.

On the other hand, if you're gone twelve hours a day a bird will not be a good pet for you, either. Birds are sociable creatures who don't do well when left alone all day. For busy people, a tankful of fish or a nocturnal hamster are much better pets. At the very least, the only bird you should consider is a small species who can be given a roomy cage and the company of other birds, such as a small group of finches. Medium and large parrots, who must live one to a cage, should not be considered unless you can take your bird to the office with you.

Finally, do you take a lot of vacations or business trips? If you're a dog or cat owner, you might automatically think of a boarding kennel, but birds are stressed too much at boarding kennels. Even a pet sitter who comes to your home may be enough of a change to depress or upset your bird. Frequent travelers should consider only those small species who can be given the company of other birds.

While you're mulling over the amount and regularity of daily time needed for a bird, remember that this daily time will have to be kept up for years.

Birds are not short-lived pets. In the old days your grandmother may have kept a succession of canaries who lived a year or two and died suddenly, but today we know how to properly feed and care for pet birds. Their life span has been greatly extended. True, finches may live only two to eight years, but canaries, parakeets, lovebirds, lories, and conures can live eight to fifteen years, the same life span as a dog or cat. Cockatiels and mynah birds can live to the age of twenty-five. And the large parrots can live seventy years—indeed, some parrots outlive their owners!

So you must look upon bird ownership with at least the same long-term consideration you would bring to choosing a dog or cat. With the vast majority of species you are looking at one to two decades of proper care and handling; with the larger species, you are taking on a lifetime of care and responsibility.

You need to consider, as well, exactly how and where a bird will fit into your household. Will you be inconvenienced by the size and placement of the cage? You must place the cage in a room with sufficient activity to keep your bird interested. Birds who are stuck in back bedrooms will not receive enough attention, and they will respond by shrieking and plucking out their feathers. The kitchen is also not acceptable, for health reasons that I discuss later. The living room, dining room, or family room are best. You'll need a well-lit corner away from direct sun, window and door drafts, heating and air-conditioning vents, and loud televisions or stereos.

Do you have room for a cage? A parakeet requires a cage about fifteen inches high, wide, and deep. Every other species, including small canaries and tiny finches, requires more room, so those little plastic cages in the pet shop are useless no matter what size bird you're considering. If you're thinking about a big parrot, a heavy-duty freestanding cage will measure three or four feet wide by two feet deep by five feet high. You'll also need room for a separate T-stand, playground, or jungle gym.

Once you've picked a suitable corner in a suitable room that offers plenty of space for the cage, consider your flooring. Carpeted rooms are not very practical for bird keeping—even the gentlest canary will happily splash his seed hulls and bathwater all over your floor and molt his feathers through the cage bars. Rambunctious parrots will fling their daily fruit and vegetables *splat!* against your walls. If the room is carpeted, are you willing to place a vinyl or plastic chair mat, tablecloth, or even a shower curtain under the cage? What do you think about protecting your corner walls with clear sheeting?

If you own your own home, then by all means feel free to allow your bird to chew up your woodwork and sprinkle his droppings on your carpeting. But if you're thinking of a bird because you rent, and your landlord doesn't allow dogs or cats, it is grossly unfair to allow your bird to destroy the place. Once the landlord discovers the extensive damage that parrots are capable of, he or she will angrily add birds to the not-allowed list, and you will have ruined it for more responsible owners.

You're surprised that birds are so messy? You've always pictured a bird as a sweet, lovely, immaculate decoration for your home? Ha-ha! All birds are messy, and some species are very messy. The first time you vacuum the carpet beneath your bird's cage, you'll hear the *tinka-tinka-tinka* of little seed hulls, pellet remnants, cucumber seeds, and cracker grains whizzing into the bag. You'll discover that a Dustbuster is one of your best friends.

With curiosity and awe you'll scoop up the first few feathers shed by your bird; what splendid coloring and softness and delicate details! But soon the novelty will wear off and you'll just pitch them wearily into the wastebasket—that is, if they're all in one piece. Some bird feathers disintegrate, creating a fine white powdery dust that floats onto your furniture. If you're allergic to feathers or dust, you should not consider a bird for a pet.

Now who's going to clean the cage? Whoever draws this chore will be wrinkling his or her nose, I assure you. Bird droppings are odd-looking things:

greenish on the bottom and whitish on the top, sometimes round and neat, sometimes loose and shapeless. If you try to avoid cleaning altogether, the cage will smell. Cleaning is a fact of life with birds. Every day or two, somebody needs to replace the newspapers in the slide-out tray. That sounds easy enough—I can see a lot of hands volunteering for this one—but newspapers don't necessarily remain solid sheets. Some birds happily shred them into a million tiny pieces and build a nest out of them in the corner of the cage.

If you protect the newspaper by covering it with a grate, the droppings clog the grate and have to be scraped off. Personally, I'd rather shovel up shredded newspaper than soak and scrub a filthy grate.

And is there anything more disgusting than cleaning a food or water bowl with droppings in it? No matter how carefully you place the perches so that your bird cannot possibly "hit" the bowls, he will find a way to do it.

Will you be irritated when your bird makes noise? He will make noise, you know. Even finches and canaries make humming noises with their wings as they flit from branch to branch. Parrots flap their wings vigorously to "practice" flying. They also clamber across the cage bars, scratch around in the newspaper, gnaw on toys and perches, and ring their cowbell. All birds chirp, twitter, sing, whistle, chatter, squawk, and/or screech. Birds are not silent creatures, by any means.

Some birds talk, and while you may think you'd love a bird who talks up a storm, a chatty mynah bird has driven more than one bird owner straight up the wall. It seems true that the better the talker, the noisier the bird is in general.

Might you be afraid of a bird? Some people don't like the idea of a free-flying bird winging his way toward them, aiming for their head or shoulder. Perhaps they remember Alfred Hitchcock's movie. Or they may not mind the flying, but are concerned about being pecked. Canaries and finches might occasionally peck a hand, it's true, and it can sting. Small parrots such as budgies and cockatiels can bite hard enough to produce an "ouch!" And large parrots such as macaws and Amazons are capable of breaking small bones.

If you haven't thrown this book aside in horror, let me explain. When I first started working with parakeets, I was assured that a bite was nothing to worry about. Gosh sakes, said the experts, puppies nip harder than birds. Sure enough, when my budgies pinched me, I laughed—ha ha!—at how foolish I had been to worry.

Then one of my females nailed me a solid bite. Ouch! I sucked in my breath, hurried to the sink, and ran my sore finger repeatedly under cold water. She hadn't even broken the skin, but the sharp indentation was shaped like a perfect U. It ached steadily for a good half-hour. Not long after, my hand strayed within reach of a scarlet macaw. His bite drew blood, and my hand turned some very interesting shades of purple and red over the next several weeks. Note, by the way, that birds have no teeth, so they bite simply by closing their beak fast and hard.

Now all this talk about biting may seem ridiculous to experienced bird owners. "Pooh!" they scoff. "Birds seldom bite when they're handled properly." This is very true. But just as experienced dog trainers forget what it's like to be a novice at one end of the leash, experienced bird owners sometimes do the same. Because they're so familiar and comfortable with birds, and can recognize their moods and "what they're thinking right now," they assume that a novice can do the same. Because they handle their birds with confidence and rapidly take charge of tricky situations, they assume that a novice will do the same.

But not all novices have the same understanding of their animals. When instructing a dog obedience class, I'm constantly amazed by the inability of owners to "read" their own dogs. What seems perfectly obvious to me about what a dog is thinking and feeling is often incomprehensible to the dog's owner. "How did you know he would do that?" they ask. "What did you see?"

Well, I'm not quite sure: a tightening of muscles, a twitch of an ear, a glint of an eye, a certain look. I think sometimes it's more what I feel from the animal. As odd as it may sound, telepathy is an important asset in handling animals. The best animal trainers not only teach and handle an animal correctly; they believe that the animal will do the exercise correctly and they visualize the animal doing the exercise correctly. Animals respond to your attitude and visualization as much as they do to your handling and teaching.

Birds may be among the most telepathic of animals, so if you confidently visualize your bird perching quietly on your hand, he is more likely to do just that. If you're worried about him biting you, he's likely to do that. "Animal people" often understand animals with an ease that escapes the average person; they are attuned to animals in ways that others find puzzling. Those bird owners who pooh-pooh the idea of biting are usually the ones with the confident mind-set that communicates all the right things to their birds. Not every novice comes equipped with that skill.

So if you feel uncertain around animals, especially around birds, you may get bitten. If you frighten or startle your bird, or suddenly stick your hand into his cage, you may get bitten. Birds are territorial creatures. They look upon their cage as their home, and they may peck at your hand if you suddenly thrust it at them. Many owners are bitten simply because they don't respect a bird's territory.

≈　　≈　　≈

Assuming your bird isn't pecking at you, what else might he do that could be difficult to live with?

Quite a few things, actually. Birds can be masters at getting into trouble, especially birds from the parrot family. They have a knack for being both frustrating and funny at the same time! For instance, it's hard to resist strangling your yellow-naped Amazon when he chews your shoes into sandals, but it's also hard to be upset when he sits perched on your computer, cheerfully bellowing, "Oh happy day, the sun is shining!" Then he deposits a dropping on your computer screen.

It's hard to spend hours teaching your Indian Hill mynah to say, "Hello, friends!" but when you proudly present him to your guests, he says, "Get out of here, you $%@*#s!"

It's hard to trim the overgrown claw of a struggling budgie. It's hard to pull out the bleeding feather of a shrieking cockatiel. It's hard to race frantically to the vet in the middle of the night because your Quaker parrot swallowed your diamond ring.

The ideal bird owner should be patient, with an easygoing attitude toward life and a sense of humor. Be honest: do you lose your temper when the blockheads around you don't understand the perfectly clear things you're telling them? Well, wait until you try to tell a bird what to do!

Put away the dream that your bird will be a feathered version of your Golden Retriever, gazing with adoration into your eyes and eager to respond to your every command and whim. Some species do enjoy cuddling, and other species do tricks, but a bird will never respond with the blind enthusiasm of a dog. Many birds have a strong will and/or a delicious sense of humor—indeed, they delight in getting into every possible mischief and in balking you at every turn.

Other birds won't get into any trouble; instead, they'll simply treat you—their loving owner—with utter indifference. Finches, for example, are happy to go about their daily business of eating and drinking and perching and flying and grooming their feathers, without ever acknowledging your existence.

So it's important to decide what type of pet you want. A bird will require as much time and patience as a dog or a cat. But a bird will not act or react to you quite like the dog or cat that you may be more accustomed to.

Even if you believe that you're up to having this type of pet, you must consider the rest of your family. Some family members may not be thrilled with the idea of a living room corner littered with seed hulls and bird droppings.

Everyone should agree that bird dirt, bird dust, bird flutterings, bird noise, and possibly bird mischief will not be a problem.

If you have children, they might be wonderful with your bird, but they also have no idea how easily a bird can be frightened or hurt. A six-year-old who runs a toy truck across the bars of the cage may panic the bird and cause frenzied flapping and wild shrieks. Some children, perhaps thinking of downy chicks or the pigeons they feed at the park, can't resist sticking their fingers into the cage to "pet" the bird or let him "sniff" their finger. Don't underestimate the tremendous power of a macaw's beak, or even the uncomfortable sharpness of a canary's.

If your home is full of toppling blocks and pretend gunfire, and of boisterous youngsters running in and out, you must choose your species carefully. Be prepared to place the cage in a safe location, and keep a close eye on the children. Observe your bird to see how well he copes with the quick movements, loud voices, and clumsiness of most children.

If you're thinking about a bird as a pet for your child, you must already know that children have short attention spans. They seldom enjoy the chores that come with owning a bird, and it usually isn't long before they begin to "forget." Just as with dogs, birds for children usually become Mom's birds. A posted schedule may help children remember their chores and stick to the responsibilities of owning a bird.

Do you have other pets? Try to look at them objectively before adding a bird to your home. Muffin may adore the kids and may not dream of hurting a fly. He may not give a second look at your bird as long as the bird stays in the cage, but a bird flapping loose on the floor will awaken the hunting and chasing instinct of almost any dog. If Tweetie is a parakeet and Muffin is anything bigger than a Chihuahua, you must make sure that good ol' Muff is safely confined in another room when Tweetie is out.

Cats are even more problematic. Some cats refuse to leave birds alone even while they're in their cage. Like Sylvester the cartoon cat, your curious kitty may persist in his efforts to mow down his own personal Tweetie. Yes, photos have been taken of the family cat lying placidly with the family cockatiel, but the camera wasn't fast enough to catch the next shot: the cockatiel suddenly flapping and flying and the cat instinctively lashing out with his claws.

You must understand the difference between domesticated traits and instincts. Cats and dogs don't have time to think when a bird suddenly acts like prey. They don't have time to call upon the domesticated part of their mind—they simply react. Your new bird will be dead before anyone even knows what happened, least of all your puzzled pet. (If your cat ever happens to bite your bird, no matter how minor the puncture, call your vet immediately. The bacteria in a cat's mouth can kill a bird.)

Ironically, the problem may be reversed with larger parrots. Big parrots can be territorial and jealous, especially if the bird came first and the other pet second. Your cockatoo or macaw may live happily with Muffin and Morris, or they may screech and threaten and tease the other pet. If the parrot gets out while the other pet is in the room, Muffin or Morris may be the ones who end up with blood on them!

If you're convinced that your home and lifestyle are suited to a bird, and all the members of your family agree, still consider the people outside your family. The biggest concern is noise. In close neighborhoods where the houses are right on top of each other, or in apartments or condos where they're actually connected, it is the height of selfishness and irresponsibility to choose a species who shrieks and screeches. Large parrots can reach an unbelievable volume of unpleasant sounds, including regular screaming at dawn and/or dusk.

There have been some disturbing stories in *Bird Talk* magazine about parrot owners who say, "Boy, is my cockatoo loud! I can hear him shrieking when I turn my car onto my street—five houses down! But I love him so much that I wouldn't give him up even if they threaten to evict me!"

This owner may think he is showing patience and devotion, but what he is expressing is utter disregard for the rights of other people. Yes, he's learned to live with the shrieking because his rewards from his bird outweigh the noise nuisance—for him. But what rewards do his neighbors receive besides a splitting headache, disrupted sleep and quiet, and an inability to work at home or entertain guests?

I can assure you that if anyone moved into the apartment upstairs from me with a screaming Moluccan cockatoo, I would call animal control with no hesitation whatsoever. Parrot owners, your rights end where someone else's begin. It is possible to enjoy birds and not disturb your neighbors; you simply choose a quiet species. If that doesn't satisfy your craving for a Moluccan cockatoo, then move to a place where you can realize your dream without intruding on the rights of others. The large parrots are wonderful creatures, but they are suited only to homes away from close neighbors.

The final factor involved in owning a bird is understanding what his needs are and what makes him tick. For hundreds of years, birds have been kept for their beauty or for their talking or singing skills, but they were not considered "serious" pets. Birds were impulse pets—throw-away pets. They lived a few years, they died, you buried them, you bought another one.

For example, your grandmother probably purchased her canary for a dollar from the pet aisle of Woolworth's. She kept him in a tiny plastic cage ("Sale! $5.99!") and every couple of days she poured seeds into his dish. For a year or two, the canary would hop around and sing, and then one morning Grandma found him lying on the bottom of the cage with his feet sticking up. She buried him in the back yard—with honest tears—and headed back to the pet aisle of Woolworth's. "Glory's sake," she would muse on the way, "canaries are such sickly creatures."

But canaries are not at all sickly when they are chosen and cared for properly. Canaries, in fact, can live up to fifteen years. Your grandmother simply didn't know how to choose and care for one.

Fortunately, today we know much more about keeping birds happy and thriving. We know, for example, that most bird illnesses aren't caused by the Virus From Nowhere. Most bird illnesses are brought on by stress, and stress is brought on by a seed-only diet, rough or careless handling, an erratic household, or a tiny or dirty cage stuck in a draft or hidden away so that the bird gets no contact with people or other birds. A bird who is "cared for" in this way will pluck all his feathers out, peck at you when you come near, scream himself hoarse, or simply wither and die.

If this is not the type of pet you want, you must learn enough about bird behavior to provide a happy home. Read up on bird behavior. Find out how birds think and why they do what they do. Two top parrot behaviorists in the country are Chris Davis and Sally Blanchard. Their writings appear often in *Bird Talk*. Don't make the mistake of assuming that a bird is similar to a dog, a cat, or a human being. You and your bird are different species. Since *you* are the more intelligent, you must learn everything you can about your bird. You must learn how to communicate in ways that he will understand. You must speak his language because he can't speak yours.

You must recognize your bird for what he is, because God created him as a wonderful, unique creature with talents and abilities all his own. It is not only incorrect but wasteful and demeaning to consider him a feathered person. A bird's thought processes are very different from ours, with basic instincts and basic ways of responding to sights and sounds. Before you can truly provide the best home for your bird, you have to understand him.

Let's take a practical, close-up look at your bird.

What does the world look like to the bird? Compared to a dog or a cat, the eyesight of a bird is extremely sharp and filled with bright colors. Birds use their excellent eyesight to study everything going on around them. Their visual memory is astounding; they can detect the slightest difference between what they see right now and what they saw an hour ago. I've already said that birds are rigid creatures that dislike change. Their keen eyesight helps them to detect this change, and this can lead to problems.

For example, when I fill my budgie's vegetable dish, woe is me if I include the tiniest piece of anything orange. She immediately climbs to the top of her cage and glares at the dish until the bit of carrot is removed. When I clean her cage, if I rehang her swing on any cage bar other than the one it hung on before, it will be several hours before she warily decides that the swing is still safe to use.

Damsel, an African grey, was extremely upset when his owner planted a flowering bush outside the window. For four days, Damsel huddled in the farthest corner of his cage, where he didn't have to look at the bush.

Marcus, a scarlet macaw, began plucking out his feathers when his owner repanelled the dining room walls. Cookie, a pionus parrot, made asthmatic wheezing sounds when her owner hung a new painting above the fireplace. Gizmo, a Senegal parrot, shrieked and flapped his wings as he stared at the roll-top desk in the den. One of the kids had innocently placed a roller skate on top of it.

Yes, birds are unusual creatures, especially parrots. You're not likely to get the same dramatic responses from canaries or finches. But always keep in mind the keen eyesight of your bird and his suspicion of change. If your bird is acting strangely, look around the room to see if anything has changed.

Also take a close look at yourself. If you come home with a grumpy expression after a run-in with your boss, don't be surprised if your bird begins to screech or peck at you or refuse to have anything to do with you. Birds are amazingly responsive to facial expressions.

New haircut? Sandals instead of sneakers? Contact lenses instead of glasses? Blue-shaded sunglasses instead of gold-shaded? Starting to grow a beard or moustache? Your parrot will probably notice, and will probably respond accordingly. It can be amusing to see his head cock and his eyes narrow with suspicion—all because the beads on his new toy are light blue rather than dark blue. But if change is overdone and if you have a particularly sensitive bird, he may end up emotionally stressed, which can lead to physical illness.

Your bird is also adept at spying sudden movement, even when he's looking in another direction. You can easily frighten a bird with a tiny and innocent wave of your hand. Birds have one eye on each side of their head, each of which sees the world independently. So if your bird is sitting in the center of your living room, he has an excellent view of the right side of the room and the left side of the room. But he can't see front or back very well. That's why he cocks his head when you're standing directly in front or behind. The eye that's facing you is busily studying every little detail about you, while the other eye is examining a completely different field of view!

What does the world sound like to your bird? Birds hear much, much better than you do: softer sounds over greater distances at higher frequencies. They have been known to act strangely immediately before an earthquake; some experts speculate that perhaps your bird can hear the far-away rumblings that precede the quake. Most birds seem to prefer the higher-pitched voices of women and children to the deeper voices of men. Most birds do not like loud sounds at all.

Does your bird think? Yes, of course he does. Parrots in particular are highly intelligent creatures. But birds are also highly instinctive; they often act first and think later. Reacting quickly to the slightest indication of a threat has saved the lives of generations of wild birds. Your pet bird retains this flight instinct; if startled or surprised, he may automatically flap or fly or bite. You must work around your bird with a steady, calm demeanor that does not incite him to react without thinking.

We've talked about money, time, attention, household stability, patience, tolerance, consideration for others, and understanding. Those are the responsibilities of bird ownership. But what do you get in return? The rewards aren't tangible, but that's the case with so many rewards of greatest value.

Your bird will offer you pride in his magnificent plumage and brilliant colors. A Gouldian finch, with his striking combination of jet black, scarlet, turquoise-blue, deep purple, golden yellow, and bright green—each color sharply delineated—is one of the most gorgeous creatures on earth.

Your bird will offer you the enjoyment of jubilant song or cheerful twitter. A male song canary stretched up on his toes, beak wide open, reaching for the high notes, may have you belting out the song right along with him. A group of zebra finches, gossiping endlessly with their *bee-bee-bee-bee*, will have you scratching your head and wondering what it's all about.

Your bird will have you whispering, "Wow! Did you hear that?" when he runs through his repertoire of phrases and whistles. "Hi, Mom!" says an eclectus parrot. "Peace on earth, the room's a mess," declares a Quaker parrot. A lutino cockatiel whistles an excited greeting as soon as you turn your key in the lock.

You will laugh at your bird's amusing tricks and stunts. A blue-and-gold macaw will turn somersaults for nothing more than a bite of your pepperoni pizza. A lively pair of pied budgies will kick a plastic sphere across your dining room table in an impressive rendition of avian soccer.

Your bird will provide a comforting link to the natural world, so often lacking in our modern lifestyles. If you provide a roomy cage filled with natural twigs, sturdy branches, and fresh greenery, a peaceful flock of society finches may build nests, lay eggs, and raise their young for you.

Your bird will offer you the opportunity for accomplishment. If he maintains shiny feathers, flies around, grooms happily, and chatters or sings with enthusiasm, you will know that you've provided a wonderful home. Such success offers great personal satisfaction that may otherwise be hard to come by.

Your bird will cheer you up whenever you need a shoulder to cry on. Birds are highly emotional and empathetic creatures who pick up on your thoughts and feelings so easily that it can be scary. If you're feeling lonely or sick, your bird will run across his perch and cock his head and say, "Hi, beautiful!" He'll run through his entire repertoire of somersaults and inside-out twists. If you're a homebound person, are grieving from personal loss, or suffer stress, your bird will give you something to live for. He needs you to take care of him.

Birds offer a type of companionship that is neither greater nor lesser, but simply different, from its canine, feline, or human counterpart. Over the years I have kept a combination of birds, dogs, cats, and small rodents in my home. I care for them in different ways, and each one offers me something different.

One German Shepherd adored me with his huge head thrust in my lap, while another loved me from afar, while a third came to me only when she was in the mood to do so! My Norwegian Elkhound provided the satisfaction of training a stubborn and energetic dog, while my spunky Chihuahua reminds me daily that keen intelligence and staunch devotion are not dependent upon size.

And lest I grow too smug about my training skills, my cat keeps me honest. Casually she winds her way through the knick-knack cabinet, leaping gracefully to the floor and strolling off with a disdainful flick of her tail. Cats do what they want and don't look back. Cats provide balance.

The playful budgies, in turn, are full of character and self-assurance. My budgie nibbles on my finger, flirts shamelessly with her reflection in the mirror, and joyfully beats up her plastic bird toys. She will seize the cap to a pen and hurl it off her playground, raising her wings and squawking a brave "Get lost!" at the defeated pen cap.

Budgies are neither dogs nor cats. Dogs beg for a juicy supper bone. Cats bat their paws against the window glass to catch a wind-blown leaf. Meanwhile, my budgie Scooter huddles in the farthest corner of her cage, glaring balefully at a tiny sliver of orange carrot in her food dish.

Birds are different. You need to weigh these differences, these wonderful rewards, and your own responsibilities before you decide to buy a bird. Is the trade-off worth it for you?

Although those who decide that this is not the pet for them are undoubtedly missing out, there are many legitimate reasons not to get a bird. And don't let a friend lay on you that classic pressure: "Don't you want to teach your children responsibility?" If you are not committed to properly caring for a bird, what you will be teaching your children is irresponsibility. If feeding and cleaning and socialization are neglected, if your bird is listed "For Sale: Cheap!" as soon as he becomes inconvenient, you will be teaching your children that the life of an animal is not worth much—that it can be used and tossed aside at whim. Many children progress from a callous and uncaring attitude toward the life of an animal to a callous and uncaring attitude toward all life.

So, you have a perfect right to decide no.

Those who decide to buy a bird should be willing and able to take on the pleasures *and* the responsibilities, and willing and able to make a commitment. And this is exactly that: a commitment to be fully responsible for the life of another living creature. If you have a child, you may already understand that this commitment requires that you love, provide, teach, share, enjoy, discipline, worry, laugh, cry, and eventually let go.

So, you think you want a bird.

Do you know for sure now?

If you've weighed the advantages and disadvantages, the pluses and minuses, the responsibilities and rewards, and come out on the yes side, we have to find the right bird for you.

Step Two

CHOOSING THE
RIGHT SPECIES

2

EVALUATING YOUR PERSONALITY AND LIFESTYLE

You don't need this chapter: you've already decided on a canary because your uncle's second wife had a neighbor whose paperboy had one, and it was a great bird. You're just going to trot down to the bird store and pick up a pretty canary. The store owner is eager to help you. Yes, sir, did you want yellow, red, orange, or white? Perhaps agate or opal slate? You do know how to feed them to keep them that color, don't you?

Ah, you don't care about color, you just want a singing canary! Did you want a warbling song or a choppy song? Do you prefer roller canaries or American singers? Perhaps a more exotic canary. How about this one with frilled feathers? With a crested cap on his head? With speckled lizard markings down his back?

You've changed your mind. You'll just buy a parakeet. Very good, sir, did you mean a moustache parakeet, a plum-headed parakeet, or a red-rumped parakeet? Oh, you meant a budgie! American or English? Green, cobalt, violet, opaline, lutino, spangled, pied, or clearwing? Did you want one budgie, or a pair? Male or female?

Choosing a bird may seem easy, and it *is* easy if your "method" is to stroll into the closest pet store, look around at all the chattering and shrieking birds of every size and color, and stammer, "Um, I'll take that pretty one there; he's kind of cute, right?"

In many pet stores, the employees may be college kids or part-timers who know little or nothing about birds. They have little guidance to offer about the "cute" nanday conure that your eye has fallen upon. Once you get your bird home, it'll be just too bad if you didn't want a feisty bird who shrieks.

Even if you had stumbled into a knowledgeable bird store, you might still feel on-the-spot as you were peppered with all the necessary questions: "Did you want a songbird or a parrot? A single bird, a pair for breeding, or will this be for a community aviary? What size bird are you comfortable with? What price range are we looking at? Who will be handling the bird? Have you had birds before? Done any reading about birds? Are you interested in singing or whistling or talking? Tell me, were you looking for a . . . ?"

You'll be groping frantically for answers, and frantic groping will never produce the true answers that you would have come up with if you'd had more time to think in a more comfortable place. The screeching bedlam of a bird store is not the place for serious thinking. You will feel out of your league, and may give in to the temptation to buy the first bird you're shown or the most colorful, just to get yourself out of the spotlight.

The worst thing you can do when choosing a bird is to base your choice on appearance. Personality and behavior are a thousand times more important. They are the critical factors to consider when choosing a pet bird.

If you want to visit a bird store before you answer all the necessary questions, go only to marvel at all the different birds there are to choose from. At a well-stocked store you'll be flabbergasted at what you see.

You'll see bright blue-and-gold birds and dull greenish birds. You'll see a majestic pink bird perched regally on a T-stand; as you walk by, he'll raise his wings and his spiky crest and his keen black eye will roll in his head to study you. You'll see a flock of impossibly tiny birds flitting restlessly from branch to branch, twittering *bee-bee-bee-bee*.

You may see only the lower half of a bird, because the top half is hidden inside a cowbell; every so often, he rings the bell with his tongue and chuckles. You may see a blue-headed bird tearing his newspaper to shreds, and a giant scarlet bird with a powerful hooked beak gnawing his wooden perch into a toothpick. You may see the thick scaly feet of birds clambering across the cage bars. You may even see birds hanging upside down from the cage roof, staring curiously at all the upside-down people.

You may have to fight off the pleading advances of a baby cockatiel anxious for a friendly shoulder. You may find yourself trying to coax "Hello?" out of an Amazon who insists upon shouting, "Goodbye!" You will hear a cacophony of shrieks, screeches, and plain old "*Awks!*"

Such a wondrous but hectic shop is not the place to ask and answer questions. It's the place to get a general feel for the different types of birds. It's also a place to look for specific birds who answer the questions you have already considered in the unpressured privacy of your own home.

Each species has a certain character. Within each species each bird will have his own personality, quirks, likes, and dislikes, but eight or nine out of ten will follow the same general character. The ninth and tenth birds may act like an entirely different species! This sounds like a good set of odds, but with the larger parrots, those odds are less certain. The larger the parrot, the greater the chance he will deviate from the general characteristics associated with his species. Still, the odds are in your favor, so general characteristics should be given great weight when choosing your species.

Some store owners will advise you to "let the bird choose *you*." But just because a bird acts a certain way in the store for a half-hour, handled daily by people who know what they're doing, doesn't mean he will act that way in your own home over a long period of time, handled by *you*. An eleanora cockatoo who kisses your face in the store may drive you crazy after you get him home and he screams morning, noon, and night because you won't let him out to kiss your face. A bird can like you without being suited to you—or to your neighbors.

Understand the importance of choosing the right species. A major cause of problems between owners and their birds is that the bird doesn't suit the owner and/or the owner doesn't suit the bird. Examples of such incompatibility are:

- a book-loving family choosing a noisy Patagonian conure
- a person who hates to clean choosing a messy mynah bird
- a boisterous youngster choosing a gentle finch

Many people choose a species because they admire its beautiful plumage. Others succumb to an irresistible classified ad: "Rare Moustache Parakeet.

Great Price, Cage Included." Still others choose a species because their aunt had one who spoke six languages.

But in a week or a month or a year these people may discover, to their dismay, that they've started an eight- to eighty-year commitment to an incompatible bird. Then owner and bird end up in a discouraging battle as the owner struggles to change the bird's natural characteristics to more desirable ones.

It's so much better to figure out what you want *first*. This becomes even more important when your research reveals that your desired bird is unsuitable to your personality and lifestyle. Pat yourself on the back! You have been fair to yourself and to your potential bird. It's an awful feeling to dislike a pet that doesn't suit you, and it twists your conscience when you have to search for a more suitable home for it. And think of how the bird must feel about this shuffling from home to home.

How about these mismatches?

- "He screams and screeches!" wails the songwriter who can't concentrate on his work. Of course he does—he's a double yellowheaded Amazon.
- "He chews up his ladders and swings!" wails the man on a budget who is constantly replacing bird toys. Of course he does—he's a bare-eyed cockatoo.
- "She's so aloof with my friends!" wails the society woman. Of course she is—she's an African grey.

These owners might curse the species as they're plugging their ears with cotton or shelling out money for another "indestructible" toy or apologizing to their miffed friends. But these birds are not doing anything wrong; in fact, they're excellent examples of their species.

As a prospective bird owner you mustn't buy the species and then try to change it. Choose the right species to begin with. The three mismatches just mentioned could as easily have been the right choices. The songwriter could have chosen a melodious Pekin robin. The man on a budget could have chosen a nonchewing canary. The society woman could have chosen an extroverted lory.

They just didn't know.

But you do. You can start your owner-bird relationship off on the right foot by evaluating yourself and your lifestyle, deciding which avian characteristics best suit you, and then choosing a species who usually has those characteristics. The questionnaire that follows asks about your wants, needs, personality, and lifestyle. Have a piece of paper handy and begin evaluating which bird species is right for you.

Of course, you might still end up with the "tenth" bird. In addition, some behaviors and personalities can be modified and controlled by careful handling and training. But it will be less frustrating all around if you start by choosing a species who is at least reasonably compatible with your wants and needs.

THE QUESTIONNAIRE

1. Do You Want a Songbird or a Parrot?

This question is really in two parts:

(a) How much interaction do you want with a bird? Do you want a bird to handle and train? Or do you want a bird to admire from a distance: to look at or listen to?

(b) What type of sounds do you want to hear from your bird? Singing? Chirping? Whistling? Talking?

Keep these questions in mind as we discuss the two general types of cage birds: passerines and psittacines. Passerines (*PASS-er-ins*) are songbirds or perching birds. Most songbirds are seed eaters, but some species within this group are informally called softbills because they prefer soft foods such as fruits and insects. Psittacines (*SIT-a-sins*) are parrots or hookbills.

Songbirds

If you look at the foot of a songbird, you'll see three toes pointing forward and one toe pointing backward. Songbirds spend a lot of time perching on branches, so this toe arrangement provides a solid grip. If you look at the face of a songbird, you'll see a straight, pointed beak. If you have seen sparrows or chickadees, you've seen songbirds. The most common songbirds kept as pets are canaries, finches, and Pekin robins.

Not all songbirds actually sing. The canary does, and so does the Pekin robin, but of the many finch species, only the singing finch and the European goldfinch have a real song. Other finches mostly warble, chirp, cheep, or twitter. When considering songbirds, spend enough time with the various species to assess what type of sounds they produce. What may be an invigorating song or a melodious warble or pleasant twitter to one person may be a sound that drives another person crazy.

When mixed and matched to suit your musical interests, songbirds can create a wonderful choir for you. Playing environmental tapes of waterfalls and running streams will encourage them to sing, as will playing tapes of other singing birds. They will improve their songs with practice, and usually sing best on sunny spring days.

With only a few exceptions, the personalities of songbirds are peaceful and gentle, quiet and nondestructive. If you are very patient, some of these small, lively birds can be tamed to perch on your finger or take seed from your hand. But most don't enjoy touching or handling. Some will barely acknowledge your existence. Songbirds can't talk, nor will they perform tricks on command, and most pay little attention to toys.

Songbirds, then, are birds to enjoy by watching and listening. Because they prefer to interact with their own kind, and because they have few behavioral problems, songbirds are the easiest all-around birds to live with. If you're away all day, a group of songbirds may be the right choice for you. If your idea of a pet bird is a small, gentle creature who sings beautifully, chirps or twitters cheerfully, comes in several lovely colors, and/or lives peaceably in a wild setting of natural branches, then a songbird is an excellent choice for you.

How many songbirds do you want? If only one, the canary is your choice, since they prefer their own cage. But this also means that your bird needs more human companionship than other songbirds. Buy a male if you want a singer; female canaries just chirp. In the canary profile (pages 72–76) you'll discover a wide choice: specialized singers, unusual colors, even exotic feathering.

If you want two songbirds, try a mixed pair (one male, one female) of Pekin robins. A few finch species also do well in pairs. If you want a group of songbirds and have room for a four-foot-long cage or small aviary room, three pairs of finches will work well. These little birds spend most of their lives chirping to each other, grooming each other, and flitting back and forth across perches or among branches. If your cage is roomier, you can add a pair of canaries. But don't add any parrots or parakeets; with few exceptions, they are too intimidating for gentle songbirds.

Songbird Caution 1: Be sure that your house has the space for a roomy cage. Songbirds are very active and require horizontal room to fly. Ah-ha, I can hear you trying to work out a compromise: you'll keep your songbirds in a small cage most of the time, and occasionally let them exercise in a larger "flight" cage brought in from the garage. This can work for parrots but not for songbirds, because the latter are too easily stressed from handling or netting.

If you build the flight cage with a door that fits directly over the door of the small cage, the birds could go through themselves, but trying to coax them out of the flight cage back into their small cage brings on stress. It's smarter just to provide songbirds with a large enough cage for natural flight.

Songbird Caution 2: Songbirds are easier to care for than parrots, but they won't thrive under all conditions. They must have food available at all times. These tiny birds have a very high metabolism that requires frequent nibbling. If nothing is available in their dish when their tiny bodies need it, you may find a dead bird when you look in the cage.

To sum up, songbirds do best with a roomy cage, frequent small feedings, and little or no handling.

One "songbird" who differs markedly from the rest is the Indian Hill mynah. Although technically a passerine (straight bill and three toes forward, one toe back) in the softbill subgroup (eats soft foods such as fruit), Indian Hill mynahs are not small and gentle, nor do they belong in a community aviary, nor do they sing. Instead, they are talking virtuosos with intriguing personalities and special care and housing requirements.

Parrots

You already know what a parrot looks like, right? A green bird with a yellow head and white eye ring, usually found perched on a pirate's shoulder saying witty things such as "Ahoy, matey!" Perhaps you even knew that Fred, the cockatoo on the television series "Baretta," was part of the parrot family.

Well, hold onto your perch because there are over three hundred parrot species. About half are natives of Australia and the South Pacific islands, while most of the rest hail from Central and South America and the Caribbean. No parrot is native to the United States or Canada.

We've limited our profiles to those parrot species who make the best pets and who are commonly available—fewer than seventy-five species. But even this small group may hold lots of surprises.

For example, many parrots aren't green and yellow. Parrots can be apple red, brilliant scarlet, cobalt blue, pearl gray, peach, violet, sky blue, snow white, rosy pink, even multicolored.

Parrots aren't always large, either. The common little green or blue bird that people call a "parakeet" (true name is budgerigar) is a full-fledged member of the parrot family. Parrots run the gamut from the five-inch parrotlet to the forty-inch hyacinth macaw. (Parrots are measured from head to tail tip.) When a big hyacinth spreads his wings, they can extend over the four-foot mark on your measuring tape!

Finally, not all parrots talk. Sorry to burst your bubble here, but many prospective owners are drawn to the parrot family because of the irresistible appeal of a talking bird. You can pay over a thousand dollars for a large parrot, care for him for fifty years, and the only thing that will ever spew from his beak is "Awk!" And, of course, the fruit that he spits out.

If you can't go by color or size or speaking ability, how can you tell a parrot from a songbird? Look at a parrot's face and you'll see why he is called a hookbill. His beak is hooked or curved downward to aid him in all the vigorous climbing he likes to do. Parrots use their hooked beak like a third foot, grasping a cage bar and pulling themselves up with ease. Similarly, their feet are shaped for climbing. Two toes point forward and two toes point backward, allowing them to maneuver their feet into agile grips. They also use their flexible toes to play expertly with toys.

In temperament and behavior, the parrot species share many characteristics. They have been described as the emotional equivalent of two-year-old children: intelligent, playful, affectionate, sensitive, impulsive, mischievous, strong-willed, jealous, possessive, prone to drama and theatrics, destructive, and loud—quite a combination of positive and negative traits!

They may not *show* you their negative traits when you're looking at them in the bird store, and therein lies the problem. Baby parrots work hard to win your heart. They roll their eyes comically at you, flop around on their sparsely feathered breastbone, raise their wings in an appeal to be picked up, and plead "Urk urk!"

A broad smile will split your cheeks and your heart will churn madly, and you will whip out your checkbook, possibly making an enormous mistake. A parrot can be one of the most demanding and challenging of all pets—a serious responsibility that can last for decades. The purchase of a parrot should be made only after careful thought and consideration.

Let's look more closely at parrots.

Compared to a nonparrot of similar size, a parrot has a larger, well-developed brain filled with inquisitiveness. These birds are so curious about the world that they must investigate everything within reach. Since they explore primarily with their beaks, most parrots are notorious chewers and nibblers who will strip off your wallpaper, gnaw beaverlike around your chair legs, and burrow enthusiastically through your clothes baskets. A typical Amazon parrot is Flower, who races around the living room floor like a roadrunner, picking up a child's toy, discarding it, and picking up another one. Her owner runs frantically behind her, trying to snatch all the toys before she gets to them.

Could you avoid this destructiveness by keeping your parrot confined to his cage all day? Yes, but caged parrots won't remain tame and friendly. If you want to be able to handle your parrot, he will need supervised playtime outside of his cage.

If you want to admire and laugh at a parrot's amusing antics, but you don't want to handle him, or if you're away from home a lot, consider a pair of parrots who will bond with each other for companionship. Budgies, parrotlets, Bourke's parakeets, lovebirds, and lories are good first birds who don't require handling. Another option is an aloof species who doesn't enjoy handling, such as an Indian ringneck. The larger parrots are out: to make satisfactory pets, all of these birds should be handled daily, and should spend several hours each day on a T-stand or playground.

Not too happy with the idea of a bird flapping around the house, chewing on your electrical cords and bombing your carpet with droppings? Yes, this can occur, but if your parrot is given plenty of time on his playground and plenty of attention and companionship, he'll probably stay pretty much where you put him. You can teach the bird to stay put by methodically returning him to the playground every time he tries to leave.

Many freed parrots actually climb into their cage and perch happily there so long as the door is left open. They seem satisfied that they can wander about if they want to. It's too much forced confinement that upsets a parrot. And be forewarned that an upset parrot will engage in bizarre behavioral problems: screaming himself hoarse, plucking out feathers, and bobbing and weaving around the cage.

Parrots are very loyal birds. One wild parrot will bond with another in a devoted, often lifelong relationship. When your pet parrot reaches sexual maturity—between one and five years of age—he will probably choose one member of your family to bond with. Depending on species and personality, he may remain friendly to the other members of the family and to strangers, or may become aloof or even aggressive toward them.

Josephine, a military macaw, had bonded with the husband in her family. Every time the wife approached the cage, Josephine would glower at her and command, "Stop staring at me, you ninny." A blue-fronted Amazon named Rosita bonded with the oldest daughter in her family. Whenever the girl was gone for more than a few hours, Rosita pleaded, "Come on, where's Ellen?"

Large parrots can be very choosy about the sex of their owner. They may adore women while refusing to be handled by men, or vice versa. This rigidity is difficult to change, and such a parrot should ideally live with the sex of owner that he or she prefers. Sometimes you'll see classified ads like this one: "Seeking Male Owner for Tame African Grey." Whether a bird prefers men or women doesn't seem to have any connection with the sex of the bird.

If birds in general are extremely observant and suspicious of new things, parrots are triply so. All the examples in the discussion of phobic reactions that some birds have when their environment is changed involved parrots. Parrots loathe change. But ironically, if parrots aren't exposed to change, they can also be difficult to live with!

For example, if you always feed your umbrella cockatoo at six o'clock when you get home from work, he may throw a screaming fit because you got tied up in traffic and didn't get home until seven. A grey-cheeked parakeet, however, may become so bored with his toys that he screeches nonstop, just for something interesting to do. Carefully structured change is important to keep your parrot both flexible and stimulated.

Parrots are also more skilled than songbirds at reading your facial expressions and body language. Many of them won't hesitate to voice their opinion of what you're doing, what you just did, and what you're going to do next. They can be bossy creatures, quick to take advantage of your lack of confidence or expertise. They can tell when you're afraid of them and when you don't know what you're doing.

For example, if you let your parrot use your shoulders and head as a climbing post, you're asking for trouble. In spite of those cute photos of shoulder-perching parrots, novices should not allow their parrots to do this. Height makes parrots feel strong and secure. If you allow them to spend much time at the same level as your face, they can get cocky and might try to clamber across your head or play hide-and-seek across the back of your neck while you grope blindly at them. They consider this "game" to be a loss of control on your part, and they will grow ever bolder and less manageable. Parrots don't appreciate your tolerance as much as they take advantage of it.

Don't allow your parrot to run up your arm onto your shoulder or to crawl across the back of your neck. Teach him to climb promptly onto your hand or onto a stick when you say "Up!" and teach him to stay there. Playing on your lap or knee is fine, as is playing on a jungle gym placed chest- or waist-high. The cage, playground, and/or T-stand should not be placed so that your parrot can look down on you, lest that be exactly what he'll do in this situation—look down on you.

Compared to songbirds, parrots are loud creatures—and I don't mean singing, because parrots don't sing. Some parrots have an admirable whistle, though. If you play "Jingle Bells" over and over, some parrots might learn how to whistle the entire song. It's not exactly "singing," but is certainly fascinating to hear.

Rather than singing, parrots substitute an ensemble of squawking, chattering, cackling, cheeping, jabbering, babbling, mumbling, muttering, and grumbling. Their natural voice may be quiet, loud, shrill, harsh, pleasant, or unpleasant.

Some parrots imitate sounds that they hear regularly, such as the ringing of your telephone, the buzzing of the doorbell, the whirring of the blender, even your dog's barking. Sounds like fun, doesn't it? Sure, just wait until the telephone rings and you scramble out of your hot bath only to discover a dial tone, while your yellow-naped Amazon shrieks with maniacal laughter.

Speaking of shrieking, the large parrots (Amazons, cockatoos, and macaws) let loose with daily periods of screaming and screeching. At dawn and dusk, when their wild counterparts would be gathering food, most large parrots begin to scream—not with anger but with sheer joy. They act as though they must express themselves or they'll burst.

Parrots also scream during the day to express displeasure, boredom, and excitement. They scream to demand attention and companionship. They scream when another pet they dislike enters the room. They scream when you have the audacity to answer the telephone or doorbell and spend time talking to someone other than them. They scream to say hello to you.

The ear-splitting racket that a large parrot can make is difficult to stop. Yelling has no effect other than to upset—or encourage—the bird. Never strike a bird for screaming—or for any other reason. Birds do not understand physical discipline. They will not connect it with the bad deed or even with their action at the moment. They will connect it with you, and they will fear you. Parrots have a very long memory. If you treat them well, they will repay you with loyalty, but if you mistreat them, they can hold a grudge or be fearful for a very long time.

Now that we've brought up the sobering reality of parrot noise, let's balance it with a more cheerful type of noise: talking. How many of us haven't dreamed of having a talking bird at one time or another? Would you like to own one?

Before you decide, it's important to understand that most of the words that a parrot says are not speech, but imitated sounds. There's a big difference.

Speaking means understanding the meaning of words, phrases, and sentences, and deliberately using them in appropriate situations. Most of the time, parrots don't do this. Instead, they imitate at random, repeating words and phrases without understanding their meaning. Chattering lories will roll onto their backs and wrestle with a tennis ball while mumbling "Apples under the dog's dish!" or "Paper towels bad bad bird!" A bare-eyed cockatoo will happily announce "Hooray, the Lakers win again!"—just as the vet is preparing to stick him with a needle.

But let's say you turn out the lights every night and say "Goodnight!" to your cockatiel. One night you turn out the lights and your cockatiel pipes up, "Goodnight!" My gosh, he's talking!

Well, not really. A parrot who uses phrases exactly as he hears them, in the exact situations he hears them in, is not really speaking. The words are appropriate for the situation, yes, but only because he has learned them that way and is repeating them in that way.

In other words, your cockatiel is filling in the blanks of a familiar routine. He's learned that lights out is always followed by "Goodnight!" Since parrots have a voice box that can create a wide range of sounds, and since they can control those sounds quite accurately, your cockatiel simply adds the goodnight without any understanding of what the word means. If you had regularly said "Pumpkin seeds!" after turning out the lights, he would probably have copied that instead.

But here's where it gets exciting! Some parrots will use appropriate words and phrases in unusual situations that have not occurred before. For example, a spectacled Amazon became highly agitated and cried "Pop Tart! Tart! Tart!" when his owner's Pop Tart became stuck in the toaster and began burning. A blue-and-gold macaw angrily screamed, "Bad dog! Go home!" when a strange dog entered the yard and began harassing the family's cat. An eclectus parrot asks for grapes or apples ("One purple grape, please!") and stubbornly rejects anything but the requested fruit.

All ready to buy a talking parrot? They're not that easy to find. All parrot species are not equally skilled at mimicking or talking. Macaws and cockatoos may cheerfully bellow out what they think they hear, but the words often come out as harsh squawks that can grate on your eardrums. Senegal parrots try hard to talk, but their voices are so high-pitched and squeaky that they sound electronically generated. Some budgies have remarkably clear voices, while others sound like tiny computers or like a 33 rpm record album played at 78 rpm!

Parrot species who are usually apt pupils and possess clear speaking voices include the African grey, the Indian ringneck parakeet, the yellow-naped Amazon, the double yellowheaded Amazon, and the blue-fronted Amazon.

Some talented members of these species can develop a vocabulary of more than a hundred words and phrases.

African greys, especially, are skilled at perfectly copying individual voices. Mind you, we're not talking about just words here, but voices. It is very spooky to hear your daughter call, "Mom, I'd like a sandwich!" and after you fix it and take it upstairs, the only daughter you find is a chuckling African grey.

Another species who is an outstanding mimic is the Indian Hill mynah bird. As we discussed earlier, he is not a parrot but a softbill passerine. An Indian Hill mynah can rival an African grey in talking skills.

Baby birds are always your best candidates for talk training, but don't weigh down a baby with the pressure of having to talk to make you happy. Not all individuals, even of a well-known talking species, will learn to talk. Your African grey may babble happily in his own language throughout his lifetime while never uttering a distinct human word. It may be lack of ability, lack of proper training, or simply laziness or confusion.

These "less gifted" birds can be just as intelligent, affectionate, and entertaining as the spectacular talkers, but if you'll be disappointed with a nontalker, don't buy a baby. Buy an older bird who has already proved his ability—if you can find one without behavior problems, which is probably why the owner was so willing to part with him in the first place!

To teach a bird to talk, you can hold formal training sessions. This means repeating something over and over until you're blue in the face, while your parrot sits there and stares at you. Then one day he may surprise you by casually saying the phrase, perhaps while you're talking on the phone or dozing off to sleep. Or he'll spout some other phrase that you said once that was never meant for anybody's ears! (It's very difficult to persuade a parrot to drop an obscenity from his vocabulary, undoubtedly because he receives such an exciting reaction whenever he says it!)

Each lesson should last about fifteen minutes and be given at approximately the same time each day. It's best to take your parrot onto your hand during these sessions, but if you do leave him in his cage, remove his toys and food cups so there are no distractions. Turn off the television and radio, and ask other family members to leave the room.

Single birds are much easier to teach than paired birds. Paired parrots are too involved with each other to be interested in human speech, though if one bird is already a talker, he may teach the nontalker to speak. Bird training records and tapes can also be used, some with greater success than others.

But formal lessons are not required to produce a talker. Many parrots simply pick up something that's part of an exciting daily routine. You enter the room and greet him with an enthusiastic "Hi, pretty bird!" The phone rings and you run to answer it with a breathless "Hello!" The doorbell buzzes and the dog barks, and you shout "Quiet!" Your parrot may learn to mimic any or all of these phrases—including the ringing phone, the buzzing bell, and the barking dog—without formal training. It may be one week, one month, or one year before your parrot utters his first word, but once that first one is out, the others will come faster.

Now that we've discussed the differences between songbirds and parrots, you should have some idea of which type of bird interests you most. Let's go through a few more questions to clarify your decision and help zero in on your final choice.

2. What Size Bird Will You Be Comfortable With?

If you've decided on a songbird, you'll be looking at small birds between four and eight inches long (except for the Indian Hill mynah). If you're interested in a parrot, you've got every size available from five to forty inches.

We've already discussed the special considerations of larger parrots, but since these birds are so special, let's sum them up. Large parrots include Amazons, macaws, and cockatoos. African greys share most of the positive traits of the large parrots, but fewer of the negative traits.

First, large parrots are expensive, starting at four hundred dollars and often exceeding two thousand dollars. Their cage, T-stand, and jungle gym are also expensive, take up a lot of room, and are real jobs to clean.

Large parrots vary so much in personality and behavior that three identical-looking Amazons from the same clutch can have vastly different personalities. It's hard to know for sure what you're getting when you buy that cute baby.

Large parrots need a great deal of daily attention, handling, and freedom. Denied these, they will shriek or pluck out their feathers, and you will have a hard time managing them. An ideal home for such a bird is one in which someone is home most of the day, perhaps working in a home office. If you own your own company, you might take your parrot to the office with you.

Even when they are happy, large parrots tend to be loud, and also to be destructive with their powerful beaks. When raised and handled properly, they adore people and would rather cuddle than bite. But if a large parrot has an unhappy background, and/or if you don't know what you're doing, he may take advantage of your inexperience and uncertainty. Large parrots can be bossy, territorial, and sometimes aggressive.

This all sounds like a great case against them, but they do have many positive traits. They have a longer life span, are more intelligent with greater reasoning ability, and have more complex behaviors than smaller parrots. Not all large parrots are good mimics, but those that are are capable of a wider range of more accurate sounds than smaller parrots. In addition, those parrots who are show-offs have an unsurpassable ability to learn and perform. Those who are cuddly and affectionate are usually *very* cuddly and affectionate.

But in general, large parrots are "too much bird" for the average family. Your choice is more likely to come from the small and medium parrots, who have many advantages. Their initial cost is usually less. They can live comfortably in a smaller cage, which means less expense and less room taken up in your house. However, just as small songbirds require a roomy enough cage for flight, small parrots require a cage large enough for climbing and playing. They also require plenty of interesting toys.

Small parrots produce smaller droppings, so cleaning is easier. They don't demand as much personal attention, and they can tolerate being left alone for longer periods of time. They don't have as many behavioral problems; and if they are noisy or destructive or nippy, their voices are less loud and their beaks less powerful. Smaller birds are less likely to annoy the neighbors, and they are more often allowed by landlords.

3. How Much Experience Have You Had with Birds?

Still yearning for a large parrot? If you have never owned a parrot before, don't start with an Amazon, cockatoo, or macaw. First become comfortable around smaller parrots and get familiar with their behaviors and requirements. In the meantime, read and learn as much as you can about the more complex behaviors of the bigger birds. Make sure you're confident enough to make decisions or to take the lead with others. A natural knack for understanding animals is a definite plus when considering the larger parrots.

The parrots I recommend as top of the line for a novice are budgies, cockatiels, Bourke's parakeets, and pionus parrots. Other fine "novice" parrots in the small- to medium-size range are grey-cheeked parakeets, lovebirds, conures, lories, Quakers, and Senegals.

4. Will the Bird Be a Pet for Your Children?

Remember that you or your spouse must be ready, willing, and able to assume all the responsibilities if and when your kids lose interest. That means *all* the responsibilities, not just pouring in seeds every day and changing the newspaper once a week. You don't want to be like Grandma, do you, with a belly-up bird in a few months? If you've allowed the kids to choose a bird from the parrot family, you should be prepared for handling and socialization on an ongoing basis.

Which species should you buy for children? Most kids are of the "hands-on" variety: they want to touch and hold. Thus, most children find songbirds boring, just as most children find a lovely aquarium full of fish boring after the novelty wears off. This is actually fortunate for the songbirds, since these gentle birds are easily startled by rambunctious children. If you do decide to keep songbirds in a home full of active youngsters, make sure the cage is protected and in as quiet a location as possible.

Kids usually enjoy parrots, but the larger parrots are much too powerful and/or strong-tempered for children. Adults who purchase an Amazon, cockatoo, macaw, or African grey should teach their children not to bother the bird. The smallest parrots—parrotlets and budgies—are too hyperactive to remain on a child's finger for very long and are better as observation birds. The mid-size parrots are more suited as children's pets; an excellent choice might be a gentle cockatiel or pionus parrot.

Do remember that all children must be taught to be gentle with all birds. Buying a tolerant, gentle species does not give your children safe license to be rough and abusive. Even a species considered to be good with children *can bite* if the bird is startled, teased, or simply in a grumpy mood.

5. What About Feathers, Tails, and Colors?

Unlike dogs, where length and type of coat and grooming requirements are important considerations, birds simply have feathers and they take care of their own grooming. All they need from you is a dish to bathe in. However, there are three plumage traits that might influence your selection of species.

The first is the *powdery down* found on cockatoos and their smaller cousins, cockatiels. This natural feature helps absorb dirt that could hinder flying, but it's a nuisance around the home because the powder floats through the air and lands on your furniture. Some of it will come off on your hand when you pet these "dusty" birds. They are definitely not good choices for an allergic or wheezy person.

Second, some species have *very long tails* that can be easily damaged when rubbed against the bars or wire of their cage. Long-tailed species include the macaws, Asian parakeets, and some Australian parakeets. To accommodate the tails, these species need a cage that is higher and deeper than cages for other comparable size birds. (Also, if you keep more than one parrot, the other parrots often delight in sneaking over and tugging on the long tail!)

The final plumage trait that may influence your choice is *color*. Birds can generally be divided into three color groups. The first group includes birds with no choice of color; they are mostly green with a bit of bright color (yellow, red, blue, white, etc.) on the head, wings, and/or tail. Examples include the Amazons, pionus parrots, most conures, and grey-cheeked parakeets. Some people find this color rather plain, while others consider it natural-looking.

The second group of birds also has no choice of color; they come in one color (or color combination) other than green. For example, the African grey is always gray with a reddish tail. The citron cockatoo is always whitish with an orange crest. The scarlet macaw is always some combination of red, yellow, blue, and green. You must be satisfied with that one color or color combination.

The third group satisfies people who prefer a choice. They enjoy choosing not only a species but also a unique color or pattern. Species who come in a variety of colors (solid, blended, shaded, patched, etc.) include budgies, cockatiels, lovebirds, ringnecked parakeets, canaries, and zebra finches.

Obviously your feelings about powdery down, tail length, and color are purely personal, and only you can determine their importance.

6. What Activity Level Are You Comfortable With?

Some people enjoy a bird who is lively and frisky, who hops or climbs or flits around or plays frequently with toys. Other people find that an active bird makes them nervous. Ironically, people who tend to be restless or fidgety themselves often do best with calmer birds. If you find yourself annoyed by inquisitive children or active dogs, you'll probably be annoyed by an active bird.

How much activity you like is as much an individual matter as is whether you enjoy a particular type of singing or twittering. One person's "active" bird may seem "dead" to another, while one person's "passive" bird may seem "hyperactive" to another. Study the various levels of activity at the bird store to find out what you like. And since activity level can differ among individual birds of the same species, such observation can also help you to choose among individual birds of a given species.

7. How Much Money Can You Spend?

Aside from the cost of cages and accessories, which may be less than one hundred up to a thousand dollars, your initial cost for a bird will run from ten to ten thousand dollars. (Zebra and society finches can cost as little as five dollars apiece, but these sociable species must be kept in groups, so you must multiply that figure by four or six.)

Within each species, prices vary wildly by age, degree of tameness, whether the bird was domestic-bred or imported (domestics are more expensive, but worth it), and whether it was hand-fed or parent-raised (hand-feds are more expensive, but worth it). Here are some general guidelines:

- Twenty-five dollars will purchase a pair of budgerigars, a single lovebird, or a group of zebra or society finches.

- Fifty dollars will purchase a cockatiel, a male canary, or a pair of singing finches.

- Two hundred dollars will purchase a mynah bird, a pair of parrotlets, or one of the common conures.

- Four to six hundred dollars will purchase one of the common cockatoos or Amazons, a pionus parrot, a pair of rosy Bourke's parakeets, or a sun or jenday conure.

- A thousand dollars will purchase an African grey or one of the common macaws.

- If you're interested in a scarlet macaw, a double yellowheaded Amazon, a Moluccan cockatoo, a rose-breasted cockatoo, or an eclectus parrot, you'll need between one and two thousand dollars. And, of course, there's always the hyacinth macaw for ten thousand!

3

CHOOSING THE
BEST SPECIES FOR
YOUR FAMILY

Okay, time to find the species that matches your unique list of desired traits! Turn to the species profiles. For each species, the chart at the top of the page will immediately tell you whether the bird is a parrot or a songbird.

Although approximate length is also given, this doesn't always give you a good idea of the true size of a bird. Size is more accurately related to your overall impression of a bird. For example, some cockatoos may be as short as twelve inches, but their stocky bodies, broad feathers, mobile crests, thick legs, and heavy beaks make them look much more imposing. In contrast, Indian ringnecks may be sixteen inches long, but much of that is tail, and the bird himself is so slender and elegant-looking that he doesn't appear to be any larger than the cockatoo.

Experience Level Needed by Owner is given as *experience recommended* (you should definitely have owned a bird before, ideally a mid-size parrot), *some experience recommended* (you should be "moving up" from an easy-care bird such as a budgie or cockatiel), or *fine for the novice* (you have never owned a bird before).

Price Range is approximate. As mentioned in the questionnaire, price depends upon whether the bird is an import or a domestic-bred hand-fed. Price also depends upon whether you're buying direct from a breeder (no middleman) or retail from a bird store. Price varies according to age and degree of tameness, and as with most everything else, prices are usually less in the South and more in the Northeast and on the West Coast.

The remainder of each profile discusses the bird's general appearance and physical features, personality and behavior, energy level, playfulness, talking or singing ability, general noise level, tendency to chew destructively or nip, any appreciable differences between the sexes, normal life span, cautions when buying, and specific care requirements. Health problems are mentioned when they are a particular problem in that species; otherwise, general health problems are covered in Chapter 10. Subspecies are also discussed, including differences in appearance and temperament.

As you read each profile, try to keep an open mind. Too many people approach buying a bird with preconceived ideas about various species. Perhaps you've already decided that you wouldn't dream of owning a klutzbird. Well, why not? Perhaps an A-bird nipped you in 1955. Perhaps your co-worker told you that a B-bird is the worst bird in the world, and he should know, because his great-aunt once had one.

If you're too quick to form an opinion based on a single experience with an A- or B-bird, you're ignoring the hundreds of experiences that were used to create these profiles. If a species has delighted hundreds of owners, he will delight you, too, as long as he is compatible with your wants and needs, and as long as he has been well-bred and well-raised. Try not to prejudge an entire species because of a single experience.

As you're making your choices, keep in mind that if several species have temperaments and behaviors that fit what you're looking for, feel free to choose the species that is most attractive to you. Problems only arise when people select a bird based solely on appearance.

Remember that beauty is only skin deep. If you choose a beautiful bird whose personality and behavior don't suit you, you will spend a lot of time disliking the bird and you'll find his beauty fading in your eyes. If, on the other hand, you choose a species with a personality that appeals to you but an appearance that doesn't, you'll be astonished, as time goes by, at how beautiful he becomes in your eyes.

Once you've found a few species that interest you, your next step is to see as many color photos as possible. Your bookstore or library should have illustrated books showing many species. Finally, you need to see the birds up close and personal, which means visiting aviaries, bird stores, and bird fairs or expos. You'll be doing that just as soon as you finish reading through the profiles!

THE SPECIES PROFILES

AFRICAN GREY

Region of Origin: Africa

Group: Parrot

Size: 14 inches

Experience Level Needed by Owner: Some experience recommended

Price Range: $700 to $900

Congo grey

PHYSICAL FEATURES

There is only one color choice, but it's lovely: gray-scalloped with a whitish face and reddish tail. There are two types of African grey: the **Congo grey** (*Psittacus erithacus erithacus*) is larger and lighter colored with a bright red tail; the **Timneh grey** (*Psittacus erithacus timneh*) is smaller and darker and has a maroon tail.

HIGHLY INTELLIGENT BUT INTROVERTED

The African grey is extremely intelligent, perhaps topping all other parrots in his ability to learn new things throughout his lifetime. However, this is not a parrot who will perform tricks on command. Compared to an entertaining "ham" like an Amazon, the African grey is neither outgoing nor demonstrative.

On the contrary, adult greys are considered shy and introverted; they usually bond with only one person and are aloof with everyone else. You cannot whisk a grey out of his cage and hand him over to a stranger. These parrots are suspicious, discriminating, and opinionated. Sometimes a grey will not tolerate men, while another will not tolerate women. Their choice of human partner has nothing to do with the sex of the parrot itself.

CONSISTENT ROUTINES

The African grey is one of the most rigid and pattern-oriented of all parrots. He is keenly observant and sensitive to the slightest change in routine. A change of ownership, a move to a new home, the purchase of a new cage (or even moving his cage to a different corner of the room), or the addition of a new baby or pet can cause a grey to huddle on the floor of his cage and brood—or worse, to begin plucking his feathers out. Days or even weeks may go by before he grudgingly accepts the new situation.

Greys must be handled with consistency to keep them happy, but they must also be gently conditioned to accept minor changes in routine. A young grey should be given a grand tour of your house when you first bring him home so that he feels secure in every room. His toys should be rotated and his playtime should vary slightly in length and time. Then he won't be so easily stressed when changes in routine inevitably occur. Stressed greys are notorious feather pluckers who can virtually strip themselves naked. Unhappy greys, especially imports, also make unpleasant growling sounds.

African greys require a roomy cage (three feet in all three dimensions is excellent), interesting toys, and plenty of consistent interaction—with occasional stimulations of change—to keep their intelligent minds occupied. Protection against loud noises is also appreciated; many owners leave a radio on all the time. African greys are not a good choice for a hectic or busy lifestyle.

KING OF THE MIMICS?

The African grey is an outstanding mimic, unsurpassed at perfectly imitating a specific human voice down to the last detail. Greys faithfully reproduce not only the words but the exact voice. Some skilled greys could literally answer the telephone or doorbell in their owner's voice, and no one would be the wiser.

The grey is also skilled at imitating sounds such as running water, your purring cat, even the hum of the refrigerator motor in your kitchen! African greys are very creative with their voices; they like to combine sounds and invent new ones.

Greys differ from other parrots in *when* they learn to talk. Most Amazon parrots, for example, learn early, while many greys don't begin talking until the end of their first year. New owners shouldn't be concerned when their five-month-old grey stares uncomprehendingly at them when they urge him to speak.

The vocal range of the grey is remarkable, with the bird moving effortlessly from a high-pitched woman's voice to a rumbling man's voice to the creaking of a door. Although most other parrot species seem to prefer women's voices, African greys favor exciting voices, whether male or female.

A grey may imitate the words spoken by a soft-voiced woman, but substitute the louder, more enthusiastic voice of the woman's teenage son.

Is an African grey the best talking bird of all? That depends on what you mean by "the best." The Indian Hill mynah can often match the grey in accuracy of specific voices, and the mynah is much more willing to talk in front of strangers. Greys are notorious for talking up a storm with their family, but refusing to utter a word when a stranger is present. Sometimes their frustrated owners must resort to tape-recording their bird's talents so that skeptical visitors will believe them!

Not all African greys will talk, however. Plenty of greys live their entire lives as pets without uttering a single word. You cannot force a bird to talk, and if you're unhappy with your grey because he is one of the silent ones, he will pick up your displeasure and become stressed and unhappy himself.

If you must have a talker, opt for an older grey who was hand-fed as a baby and is already talking. But remember that greys are not very adaptable, and it might be a long time before your "talking" grey opens his mouth in his new home.

NOT VERY NOISY

Compared to other parrots, African greys are not considered noisy. Because they enjoy playing with their voices, they may make high-pitched, irritating sounds, but most are not daily screamers like Amazons, cockatoos, and macaws. When upset, greys don't tend to shriek their displeasure; instead, they sulk or pluck their feathers.

BABY HAND-FEDS IF POSSIBLE

Your best choice for a pet is a three-month-old African grey who has been domestically bred and hand-fed. These birds make such wonderful, affectionate pets that it's foolish to opt for lower prices for an imported bird.

Imported greys and older domestic-bred greys who have never been tamed are not recommended as pets. It takes them far too long to adjust to new situations and new people, and many never really settle down and trust people. Many have an unreliable temperament and can bite without warning.

So opt for a young hand-fed every time. Young greys have black eyes, which change to ash-gray at several months, and then to pale yellow at one year. There doesn't seem to be much difference in the temperament and behavior of males and females, but if you're interested in a particular sex, young male greys are often darker, with larger, flatter heads and heavier beaks.

CONGO VERSUS TIMNEH

Timneh grey

Timnehs are less expensive than Congos because they are not so much in demand. People seem to prefer the lighter color and larger size of the Congo, but, actually, Timnehs are more easygoing and less moody. Otherwise, both varieties have the same talking skills and very similar temperaments. If you're ready, willing, and able to provide a stable environment for an African grey, feel free to choose either a Timneh or a Congo.

HEALTH PROBLEMS

African greys are susceptible to a seizure syndrome caused by low calcium levels. Their varied diet must include sufficient calcium to keep their body levels up.

IN GENERAL

Because greys are not as large as the other big parrots, nor as noisy or destructive, they are popular pets, and deservedly so. People often choose greys because they want one of the "major talking parrots" and the others seem too intimidating. Greys are gentler and not as threatening.

That can be fine if you're looking for a one-on-one companion rather than an outgoing family bird. It can be fine if you find a grey who interacts well with you and bonds to you. Just remember that to truly have a magnificent pet grey, you must take special care to keep his life both interesting and stress-free. Also remember that African greys can live forty to seventy years— they are a lifetime responsibility.

AMAZONS

Region of Origin: Central and South America

Group: Parrot

Size: 10 to 19 inches

Experience Level Needed by Owner: Experience recommended

Price Range: Most common species run $400 to $600

Yellow-crowned Amazons

PHYSICAL FEATURES

Amazons—the traditional "pirate's parrot"—are the most common large parrots kept as pets. Amazons are predominantly green, with blue, red, yellow, and/or white markings on their head. The various combinations of head colors distinguish the species and varieties.

EXTROVERTED ENTERTAINERS

Since there are so many species, each with a distinct temperament and behavior, it's difficult to generalize about this group of birds. Most Amazons have complex personalities, often combined with drastic mood swings, but two from the same clutch can have very different personalities. With Amazons, it's especially important to match your own personality to that of an individual bird.

It's probably safe to say that most Amazons are extroverts. They are often great showmen who love to ham it up before an audience, and it makes little difference whether the audience is made up of family members or strangers. Amazons love human company and human attention. They may not be very cuddly, but they're entertaining and demonstrative in a rather rowdy way.

Their affection can take the form of jealousy, in that they don't like their special person paying attention to anything else. That includes spouses, guests, and other pets—even talking on the phone may be protested by your Amazon. And note that Amazons "protest" with loud, demanding shrieks!

Amazons can be funny to watch when they walk because they have a clumsy waddle, but show them a playground or bird gym and they become incredible climbers who will twirl and hang and spin with amazing dexterity. These clever parrots love performing complex tricks and are frequently trained as circus birds.

For all their acrobatic skills, though, Amazons are not hyperactive. They are playful and animated, but can also be lazy. Unless fed moderately and encouraged to exercise in a three-foot-square cage, they are more prone to obesity than the other large parrots, and that leads to health problems and a shortened life span.

Good Mimics

Amazons vary widely in speaking ability, but as a group they are considered the third-best talking bird, behind African greys and Indian Hill mynahs. Some species make consistently better talkers, but within each species, every Amazon is truly an individual. Some birds will develop an impressive vocabulary of a hundred words or more, but most seem more limited. Many Amazons are more skilled at singing, whistling, and imitating sounds than human voices.

Even the skilled talkers do not mimic actual voices. Everything they say is clear and distinct but parrotlike, and they seldom drop their natural parrot harshness from their repertoire.

Noisy Screamers

Harsh is a good word for Amazons because these parrots can be very noisy. They will become neurotic screechers if confined too much to a small cage and not given plenty of attention and interesting toys.

Unfortunately, whether confined or not, most Amazons engage in daily periods of screaming. Every day, usually at sunrise and/or sunset, they shriek wildly and joyfully. This racket can last anywhere from a few minutes to a half hour, so if you are an apartment dweller or a lover of peace and quiet, an Amazon is not a good choice for you.

COMPARED TO OTHER
LARGE PARROTS

Amazons are confident, dominant parrots who know their own minds. They strut boldly around and don't hesitate to assert themselves. They are full of life and can be amusingly rambunctious, but they are also prone to crankiness and moodiness. When playing, Amazons can get overexcited, shrieking and flapping their wings wildly. I have heard this referred to as "Amazon overload." If this occurs, you should try to remove whatever toy has "gotten them going," but be cautious because in his excited state, the bird is not always thinking clearly and could bite.

Compared to African greys, Amazons are physically and mentally tougher and more adaptable. They recover more quickly from stress. When they're upset, they are more likely to shriek angrily than to brood silently and pluck their feathers. Like African greys, though, many Amazons show a marked preference for people of a particular sex, sometimes even showing hostility to people of the opposite sex.

Compared to cockatoos, Amazons will certainly chew, but they are not nearly as destructive. Although all parrots require supervision when free of their cage, Amazons are less likely to climb down from their T-stand and wreak havoc in your house. And although Amazons can be excruciatingly loud, they are still not as loud as cockatoos!

UNPREDICTABLE AMAZONS?

Amazons have a reputation for becoming pushy and aggressive when they mature at three to five years of age. Many previously happy owners become extremely discouraged with their Amazon at this time. This reputation is subject to hot debate among fanciers, but the phenomenon seems most noticeable during the breeding season, especially in male Amazons. Yellow-napes and double yellowheads seem to be the worst culprits.

Like other large parrots, Amazons get angry when their mate rejects their flirtatious behavior, and if you're the one they've chosen for their "mate," you could be bitten when you push them away. Fortunately, when excited, nervous, or upset, most Amazons give warning before biting: they dilate or "flash" their eyes by rapidly expanding and contracting the pupils. They may also fan out their tail and raise both wings above their back.

As with all parrots, domestic hand-feds are your best choice. Unfortunately, Amazons don't breed in captivity as readily as do other large parrots, and since so many Amazons are legally imported and offered inexpensively, there is little incentive for American fanciers to breed.

In the future, when all importing is prohibited, this unhappy situation will change and perhaps the characteristic Amazon moodiness will change with it. For now, though, you must be careful to avoid imports. They may be hundreds of dollars cheaper than domestic hand-feds, but they are risky propositions. It takes a great deal of time and patience to tame imports, and many will never really trust humans.

You also should be on the lookout for Amazons who have been smuggled in, bypassing the USDA quarantine stations and bringing all their illnesses (Newcastle disease, psittacosis, and parasitic infections) and wild behaviors with them. Since Central and South America are so close to the United States, and since many Amazon species are endangered in the wild and may not be legally imported, smugglers see a quick and easy way to make a buck. Legal imports are stressed and suspicious birds, but smuggled birds are even worse. They have been tossed around and shuffled through the greediest and most uncaring hands possible.

I hope this has convinced you to happily spend the money for a domestic hand-fed Amazon with a closed band on his leg. (An open band was put on by the quarantine station and signifies an import.) Young hand-feds have known nothing but love and gentleness from humans. Look for the dark flecks on the beaks of young Amazons and their dark eyes; older birds have yellow or orange eyes. Youngsters also have duller coloring because it takes years for an Amazon to develop his full adult plumage.

In General

Amazons can live sixty to seventy years. There seems to be some confusion about the common names of the species, with some species going by several common names. Always ask the scientific name so you know for sure which Amazon you're buying.

Mealy Amazon (*Amazona farinosa*)

At nineteen inches, the mealy is the largest Amazon commonly offered as a pet. Despite his size, this easygoing bird is one of the gentlest and easiest to handle of all Amazons. Because he's rather plain-looking, he is vastly under-rated as a pet, and this is a shame, since the mealy is consistently docile and mild-mannered. Some are fair mimics, but their powerful voices are also capable of ear-splitting shrieks. Thus, they make delightful pets—if you live far enough from the neighbors.

The mealy takes his name from his unusual plumage: his green feathers have a grayish cast that creates a powdery or "mealy" appearance. He also sports a large white ring around each eye, giving him a curious, innocent look.

Double yellowheaded Amazon
(*Amazona ochrocephala oratrix*)

This Amazon is so-named because he wears a hefty chunk of yellow on his head. He is a deservedly popular pet, but so fre-quently imported that you must be doubly careful to choose a domestic hand-fed rather than an import. These are good-size birds—sixteen to eighteen inches—with equally big voices.

Along with a reputa-tion for boisterousness and screaming, the double yellowhead is an excellent mimic. He is also prized for his trainability; he loves to show off with wild silly behaviors that can appear intimidating to novices. Double yellowheads are noisy and energetic, and they require more attention from their owners than some other Amazons. Some are outgoing with everyone, while others are rather moody with strangers.

Yellow-naped Amazon
(*Amazona ochrocephala auropalliata*)

The yellow-nape is another large (sixteen to eighteen inches), popular, and commonly imported Amazon, so be sure you're looking at a domestic hand-fed. A yellow patch develops on the back of this bird's neck at about one year of age.

The yellow-nape narrowly edges out the double yellowhead as the most consistent Amazon talker. Like the double yellowhead, though, he is loud and boisterous, and can be moody. If you're going to encounter behavioral problems with your Amazon, it's most likely to occur in either the double yellowhead or the yellow-naped.

Yellow-napes are so affectionate and bond so closely with their owner that they are jealous of everyone else. This is not as wonderful as it sounds, though, because Amazon jealousy can take the form of screaming fits whenever anyone or anything diverts the owner's attention.

Yellow-crowned Amazon (also called single yellowhead)
(*Amazona ochrocephala ochrocephala*)

The yellow crown of this Amazon extends from his cere to the middle of his head. He was once very popular, but today for some reason he does not seem to be offered for sale as frequently as double yellowheads and yellow-napes. This is a shame because the yellow crown is a gentler, less excitable Amazon than the other two. He usually learns to talk and makes a good pet.

Blue-fronted Amazon (*Amazona aestiva*)

Moving to mid-size Amazons (thirteen to fifteen inches), the popular blue-front wears both blue and yellow on his head, sometimes combined with white. The amount of blue varies tremendously, from just a few feathers to a huge patch.

The blue-front is the third outstanding mimic of the Amazon family, often developing a very large vocabulary. Most are also great entertainers, clever and amusing. The blue-front is not as demanding as the double yellowhead and yellow-nape, but although most are mild-mannered, some can be nippy.

Orange-winged Amazon (*Amazona amazonica*)

The orange-wing resembles the blue-front, but never has white head feathers. He's not as popular as the blue-front, perhaps because he does not develop as large a vocabulary, but is often calmer and more friendly.

Red-lored Amazon (also called yellow-cheeked)
(*Amazona autumnalis*)

The colorful red-lored Amazon combines red and blue on his head, with yellow cheeks. He is very popular, but also very loud, and his talking ability is fairly good.

Mexican redheaded Amazon (also called green-cheeked)
(*Amazona viridigenalis*)

The Mexican redhead is considered quite the pest in Mexico because he forages through crop fields. Because Mexico is so close to the U.S. border, you must be wary of smuggled birds. This Amazon is picked out by the big red patch on his crown, while his cheeks are green to match the rest of his body.

Hand-fed redheads are quite different from the Amazons we've been discussing. Most Amazons are bold and pushy, but the redhead is basically shy and mellow. He tames nicely and shows fewer behavioral problems than the others. During breeding seasons, he'll become typically restless and nippy, but seldom will he go completely haywire like the others. Redheads are less demanding of constant attention and more likely to play happily with their toys. Some are noisy, while others are quiet. Most do not make particularly good talkers, but they can be good at imitating sounds.

Lilac-crowned Amazon (*Amazona finschi*)

The small lilac-crown is another Amazon who is more shy and mellow than bold. He is not normally a gifted talker, but some hand-feds can surprise you with unexpected talent. With his red-and-blue head, the lilac-crown looks like several other Amazons and is often sold under the wrong name.

Spectacled Amazon (also called white-fronted)
(*Amazona albifrons*)

The smallest of the Amazons at only ten inches, this engaging little bird is bold to the point of rashness. He is fearless with birds much larger than himself, and can be nippy with people as well; some can bite quite hard. Spectacled Amazons are not outstanding talkers, but they are excellent screechers, especially when you don't spend enough time with them. Most owners have no trouble spending this time, though, since these spunky birds are so much fun to watch!

This Amazon is easily distinguished by his small size and by his two namesakes: the red spectacles around his eyes and the white patch on his forehead. The species is frequently imported, so make sure you're buying a domestic-bred.

Derbyan parakeet and moustache parakeet

ASIAN PARAKEETS

Region of Origin: Southern Asia, India, and Africa

Group: Parrot

Size: 14 to 20 inches (including the extremely long tail)

Experience Level Needed by Owner: Some experience recommended

Price Range: $50 to over $300

PHYSICAL FEATURES

Most Asian parakeets are grass green or pastel green with long tapering tails. Various species will have other stunning color variations as well. Their smooth feathers give them a sleek appearance that makes them stand proud and poised; Asian parakeets are outstanding show winners.

DAILY HANDLING IS A MUST

Asian parakeets include some of the earliest pet birds kept by humans. Today, however, they are considered pests in their native countries, with huge flocks raiding orchards and plantations. These parakeets are clumsy on the ground, but agile climbers through the thickest woods. When natives try to catch them for export, they clamber skillfully into the highest branches. Remember this if your Asian parakeet escapes from his cage!

Since most cages are too cramped for them and their tails are easily damaged by the wire or bars, Asian parakeets are more popular as aviary birds than as house pets. But if you can provide a spacious enough cage and would like a stand-offish parrot who doesn't require handling, they can make satisfactory pets.

Most Asian parakeets are not affectionate cuddlers. If you plan on handling them at all, you must purchase a young hand-fed and reinforce his tameness with daily handling. Without daily interaction, these birds revert quickly to a wild state and will bite. When handling them, keep in mind that, unlike cockatiels and Amazons who ruffle their feathers and enjoy being scratched back and forth, you must always stroke Asian parakeets in the direction of their smooth feather growth. These birds dislike having their long tail touched.

Good Mimics

Asian parakeets are usually talented talkers and whistlers, especially ringnecks. For mimicking skills, males are the best choice, but Asian parakeets are difficult to sex until their adult plumage comes in at two years of age. Fortunately, there always seem to be more males than females of these species, so your chances of getting a male are good. Do note that some of these parakeets use their powerful voices for screeching.

Ringnecked parakeet (*Psittacula krameri*)

Indian ringnecked parakeet

The most popular species of Asian parakeet, this elegant bird is about sixteen inches from head to tail, and is distinguished by the black and rose collar worn by the adult male. Along with the normal green shade, beautiful color mutations include lutino (yellow), blue, pied, albino, cinnamon, and gray.

Ringnecks are intelligent birds who learn quickly and can be encouraged to perform complicated tricks. However, many ringnecks do not enjoy being house pets. Even hand-feds can be nippy, especially females. Too many people buy a ringneck because of his deserved reputation as an excellent mimic, but this species is usually happier as a beautiful, entertaining showpiece in an aviary. They have exceptionally clear voices and can develop amazingly large vocabularies. Their speech is not usually as clear as an African grey or Amazon, but it's better than that of most other parrots. They also imitate sounds and whistle tunes. Males make the best talkers.

Tame ringnecks seldom resort to their loud parrot voices, but if they are teased or neglected, they may shriek. These hardy birds live a very long time and make beautiful, entertaining pets.

There are two geographical varieties; the **Indian ringneck** is far more popular than the **African.** Prices vary from fifty dollars for the normal green color, to over three hundred dollars for the blue mutations.

Alexandrine parakeet (*Psittacula eupatria*)

At twenty inches and with similar coloring, this species looks like a larger version of the ringneck. Alexandrines will talk, but they are especially noted for their powerful shrieks and equally powerful beaks. They're usually friendly, so they don't use their beaks for biting, but for chewing. Alexandrines can be so destructive that they are often kept in metal-framed aviaries.

Moustache parakeet (*Psittacula alexandri*)

This green bird is smaller than the ringneck. He can be identified by his blue-gray head, his pink breast, and his namesake—a broad black marking that resembles a moustache. When obtained young, the moustache parakeet is outgoing, animated, and easy to tame. He will talk, but can sometimes be a bit loud.

Plum-headed parakeet (*Psittacula cyanocephala*)

Of all the Asian parakeets, this gorgeous species has the quietest voice, usually no more than a pleasant twitter. He will talk, although in a high-pitched electronic-sounding voice. He's also the least destructive of the group.

Plum-heads are handsome birds with colors so sharply separated that the bird looks painted. The male stands out with his lovely purplish head. Remember, though, that this plumage does not appear until after two years of age. Since only young plum-heads are suitable as house birds, you're better off buying young and taking your chances on which sex you're getting.

AUSTRALIAN PARAKEETS

Region of Origin: Australia

Group: Parrot

Size: 9 to 16 inches

Experience Level Needed by Owner: Bourke's parakeet and red-rumped parakeet are fine for the novice, while some experience is recommended for the other species

Price Range: $100 to $300

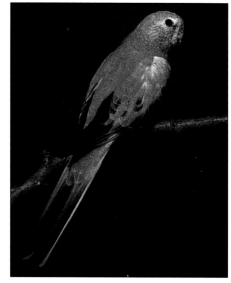

Rosy Bourke parakeet

PHYSICAL FEATURES

This group includes several plain-colored species, as well as some of the most brightly colored of all parrots. They are sleek, fast-flying birds with a heritage of flying free over broad savannahs and grasslands. Some species have long tapering tails, while others have broad scalloped tails.

MAINLY AVIARY BIRDS

Many species of Australian parakeet, although wonderful aviary birds, are unsuited to house caging; they don't tame well and are too active to settle down to life in a small cage. Several Australians, however, are comfortable as house pets if kept in a cage that is two to three feet in all three dimensions. They can be good choices if you're looking for a quiet, pretty, independent parakeet who is easy to keep and happy to do without constant human attention. But if you're looking for an outgoing, affectionate, trainable, perhaps even talking bird, you won't find him here.

Bourke's parakeet (*Neophema bourkii*)

This small nine-inch species may be the best pet of all the Australian parakeets, a great beginner's bird. Sometimes he is called a grass parakeet.

Although plain looking, he makes a great house bird: gentle, undemanding, and easily tamed. He is not a chewer, and his voice is soft, mostly little whistles and tweets, along with a low warbling song. The Bourke is not a talker. Price is less than a hundred dollars.

If all this sounds perfect, but you want something with a little more color, the **rosy Bourke** may be just what you're looking for. Heavily suffused with pink, this lovely bird commands a higher price—up to two hundred dollars—but most Bourke owners feel that he is worth every penny.

Red-rumped parakeet (*Psephotus haematonotus*)

At ten inches, this greenish species is another good choice for beginners. He is an even better choice if you're planning an aviary room rather than a cage. The red-rump is perky, easy to keep, and has a quiet cooing voice and a melodic song. He is also a wonderful foster parent, eager to raise the young of other species. With his bright red rump, the male is easy to pick out. The red-rump can be purchased for under a hundred dollars.

Barraband's parakeet (also called Superb parrot) (*Polytelis swainsonii*)

More a mid-size at twelve to fourteen inches, this lovely species combines a bright green body with a bright yellow head and rich red throat. Hand-raised babies have pleasant personalities and are not difficult to tame. Cost approaches three hundred dollars.

Rosella (*Platycercus species*)

Golden-mantled rosella

There are many rosella species, most of which are ten to fourteen inches long and brightly colored, with broad scalloped tails that can be fanned out into huge fingers. Rosellas look like the splendid tropical birds that everyone imagines should live in the jungle. Often their plumage is a gorgeous spangled mixture of four or more brilliant colors.

Unfortunately, rosellas are mainly aviary birds. Honest breeders admit that eight out of ten of their hand-fed rosellas won't tame well enough to make good pets. Rosellas are gentle (especially when young), but also independent and flighty—they just don't enjoy being handled or played with. If you do keep a rosella as a house pet, you should provide a roomy cage about three feet in all three dimensions. These birds need room to flap their wings, climb, and engage in acrobatics. They also like to run and fly, so some free playtime would be appreciated, but watch them while they're out—they are big chewers.

Most rosellas are not talkers, but they can be excellent whistlers, often learning to wolf-whistle. They are hardy and long-lived, up to thirty years. Popular rosella species include the golden-mantled, crimson, northern, eastern (or golden-mantled), and western (or stanley). Rosellas usually cost around three hundred dollars.

Princess of Wales parakeet (also called Alexandra's parrot)
(*Polytelis alexandrae*)

A big fourteen-inch parakeet with an extremely long tail, the lovely Princess of Wales features glorious pastel shades— sky blue, yellow, gray, green, and pink —all on the same bird! This species prefers walking around to flying, and is usually docile and nondestructive. Young hand-feds may remain tame, so if special accommodations can be arranged for his tail, the Princess of Wales can make a pleasant pet. Be prepared to spend around three hundred dollars.

Rock pebbler (also called Regent parrot)
(*Polytelis anthopeplus*)

Largest of all parakeets at sixteen inches, the handsome rock pebbler is olive green with a pink throat, red beak, and gray-blue head. He is gentle, may mimic a few words, and does not tend to be destructive. The only drawback is his extremely long tail, which is easily damaged in a conventional cage. If you want to keep one of these long-tailed birds as a house pet and still be a responsible bird owner, you'll need to buy or build special accommodations. Cost approaches three hundred dollars.

BUDGERIGAR
(Budgie)

Region of Origin: Australia

Group: Parrot

Size: 7 inches

Experience Level Needed by Owner: Fine for the novice

Price Range: $10 (normal green or blue) to $25 (fancier colors)

Blue budgie

PHYSICAL FEATURES

This is the bird everyone thinks of when they think of a parakeet: the little green or blue bird offered by every pet shop. But if you've read the profile on Australian parakeets, you know that the budgerigar (*Melopsittacus undulatus*) is simply one of many parakeets from Australia. However, he makes such an outstanding house pet that he deserves his own profile.

When this species first came to America, he was called a shell parakeet because of the wavy lines on his back and wings. Later, the name used by Aboriginals was discovered—budgerigar. The nickname parakeet stuck, though, and even pet-shop employees may look uncertainly at you when you ask to see their budgies. "You mean our parakeets?" they'll say.

The most obvious physical feature of a budgie is the incredible variety of colors available. The normal wild budgie is green with a yellow face and wavy black lines on his head, back, and wings. Until the early 1900s, when you purchased a budgie, green was your only choice.

Today you can choose the normal green, cobalt blue, sky blue, violet, white, gray, and yellow (called lutino). Sometimes the wavy markings are cinnamon brown rather than black. Sometimes the markings are absent on the back of the neck (called opaline). Sometimes the markings are absent on the wings (called clearwing).

A yellow face continues to be the norm on green budgies, while blue budgies usually have a white face; however, some breeders have produced yellow-faced blues. A color mixture called pied (a blend of green and yellow or blue and white patches) is popular and often offered by pet shops as an "exotic" color. A lovely color mixture called spangled (normal color pattern is reversed, with white spots and bars and black outline) is difficult to produce correctly, so it is usually more expensive.

Understand, though, that an "exotic" color is not the same as a show budgie. Show birds must wear colors of specific proportions, and the bird himself must be a precise physical type. Another distinguishing factor between pet and show budgies is the ring of spots on the underside of a budgie's throat. Proper budgies have clearly defined spots of jet black or rich brown, while "less proper" budgies have loose markings running together without forming definite spots.

THE MOST POPULAR PET BIRD IN THE WORLD

The budgie's history is astounding: he literally came out of nowhere in 1843 to capture the hearts of millions of novice bird owners. In Australia, huge flocks of wild budgies flew over dry fields searching for grass seed, their numbers so great they blocked out the light of the sun. From that humble environment, the budgie was introduced to England by the great naturalist and wildlife artist, John Gould.

Today the budgie is the most popular pet bird in the world, the bird that almost every fancier starts out with, or at least owns at some point in his or her life. For how can anyone be a true caged-bird lover without experiencing the delightful antics of this little fellow at one time or another?

AMERICAN OR ENGLISH?

There are two types of budgie: **American** (the common one seen in pet shops) and the **English** (the classic show bird, which is much harder to find).

Once you've seen the two types side by side, you can easily pick out the English. He is larger and stockier than the American. He perches ramrod-straight, his head large, his brow sculptured, his round chest proudly thrust out, his beak tucked down into his chest. In temperament, the English budgie is less feisty and more reserved. Those who like their budgies lively and agile might call the English phlegmatic, while those who appreciate the calmer English personality might think him docile. Depending on your own personality, either type makes an excellent pet.

English budgies do seem to have a shorter life span (seven or eight years) compared to Americans (eight to twelve years).

There are so many budgies being bred today that it's hard to generalize about temperament. Most budgies are lively, playful, and entertaining. If you're thinking of a placid little bird who sits quietly on a perch, a budgie is not for you.

Some budgies are mischievous or stubborn little devils, while others are sweetly amusing. Some are hyperactive, hopping and climbing all over their cage, while others are not quite so dynamic, yet will still perform an engaging repertoire of twists and flips. Most pet-shop cages are far too small for budgies. For one or two budgies, you should buy or build a cage that is at least eighteen inches in all three dimensions.

Budgies are extremely clever little birds. They delight in making up and playing games. The toy section of your pet shop was created mostly for budgies—they will play for hours with swings and ladders, plastic balls, mirrors, bells, even interlocking plastic rings that they climb through like miniature Olympians. They particularly enjoy sitting or sleeping with their heads stuck up inside a clapper bell!

Budgies vary in their attitude toward people. Most can be finger-tamed, but although some thrive on being played with, others remain rather aloof. Some will even pinch you sharply if you handle them too much, and even sociable budgies don't usually enjoy caressing. In any case, most budgies are too lively to remain perched on your finger for very long. Keep in mind that you don't have to handle your budgie to enjoy his company and antics.

Active budgies love exercise and should ideally have a playground available with swings and ladders. One playground session per day would make a wonderful life for your budgie. As he is playing happily, you can pat yourself on the back for being an outstanding budgie owner, because the majority of budgies are not so lucky as yours!

High-Pitched Talkers

Some budgies are quick to pick up words and phrases, while others never say a word. Unfortunately, even those with an impressive vocabulary can be hard to understand, since their voice is high-pitched. Budgie owners sometimes overrate their bird's speaking ability, much as new parents fawn over their baby's garbled words.

Young budgies are your best choice if you want to teach them to talk, but even that is no guarantee. I've worked with young hand-feds for months with no success. Most fanciers believe that males are more proficient talkers than females, but other fanciers insist that some females can talk rings around some males.

But most fanciers agree that if you want a talking budgie, you should keep only one. A pair become so involved with each other that they seldom bother to give up their natural chatter in favor of human sounds. The exception is if one of the birds is already a talker; then the nontalker may learn from the talker. If you must have a talker, buy an older budgie who has already proved himself, assuming you can find one for sale. Find out why he is for sale—he may be a confirmed biter!

FWEEP! FWEEP!

One or two budgies will chatter, chirp, squawk, and make a high-pitched "*Fweep! Fweep!*" but rarely is the sound loud enough to be annoying. It's not going to bother the neighbors. With several budgies, though, the harsh chattering could get on your nerves, especially if your taste leans toward musical songbirds.

MALE OR FEMALE?

Female budgies are generally the nippiest ones, and when they do bite, they bite much harder than males. Females can also be very "nesty," tearing up and shredding paper and cardboard. Even single females often lay eggs, although of course these are not fertile. Males are usually friendlier and more mellow.

Adult budgies of most colors can be easily distinguished. Their nostrils are housed in a round fleshy structure called a cere. In adult males, the cere is usually dark blue, while in adult females, it is beige or brown. Unfortunately, some of the exotic colors don't follow this indicator; and in any case, the indicator is of no use with baby budgies because the cere is usually pinkish in both sexes.

Experienced fanciers with high-quality birds may be able to distinguish male babies from female babies by the shape of the cere and head, and by behavior. As we discussed, the hardest biters are probably females!

YOUNG OR OLD?

The advantages of the male in both temperament and talking ability would seem to suggest that you should wait until the budgie's cere has changed color so that you can be sure it's going to be blue. Since older budgies are not that difficult to tame, this can work fine, but if this is your first bird and you want the easiest taming possible, you should buy a baby budgie between six and twelve weeks old.

At this age, the cere should not have changed color and there should be dark wavy lines (called color bars) covering his head and forehead right down to his cere; these fade off the forehead at maturity. Again, this does not always hold with the more exotic colors. Finally, baby budgies have solid black or red eyes, while older budgies have white circles around a dark pupil.

Unlike the larger parrots, most budgies are parent-raised rather than hand-fed. The low prices that budgies bring to breeders mean that hand-feeding is simply not worth the extra time and effort to them. Hand-fed budgies are incredibly tame and fearless, so it pays to ask for them, but most budgies are easily tamed even when parent-raised. You needn't worry about imports, since Australia prohibits the export of its wild birds. All budgies are domestically bred.

DOES COLOR AFFECT TEMPERAMENT?

This is the same question debated by cockatiel and lovebird fanciers. Some fanciers feel that birds of the newer color mutations are smaller in size and sometimes not as stable and/or hardy as those of the "normal" or original colors.

This position has logic behind it, since breeding for new colors means that the choice of parents is limited. You must stick to those birds who can produce the specific colors you want, and sometimes temperament and behavior are given a back seat to color, at least until the color is well-established.

So you might find that some color mutations are more high-strung and/or do not live quite as long as the normal color and the more established mutations. This means that greens and blues are your best bets to fit the normal budgie temperament. It doesn't mean that the other colors aren't good pets, and I personally prefer the coloration of spangled and pied budgies.

HEALTH PROBLEMS

Budgies are prone to quite a few health problems, including abscesses above their eyes and under their feet, thyroid disorders that cause breathing difficulties, and disorders of the cere. If your male's blue cere should turn brown, he may be suffering from reproductive cancer. In both males and females, the cere sometimes develops a buildup of brown skin; since this covering could eventually block the nostrils, it should be removed by your vet. The condition should especially be watched for in female budgies since their cere is normally brown, and the buildup may go unnoticed until it is too late.

"Fat" budgies should always be examined by your vet because tumors can produce swellings in the stomach and chest, and thyroid disorders can also cause obesity. You don't want to cut down the food of a bird who is ill, not fat.

In General

Budgies are the easiest of all parrots to care for, but this hardiness is too often abused. Budgies are popular impulse buys chosen by prospective pet owners with little or no previous thought or knowledge about birds. The poor little budgie then suffers dreadfully from neglect and mismanagement. Because he is tough, he may survive for quite a while under poor conditions, but he won't thrive and certainly won't be happy. When properly cared for, budgies live about eight years, but their life span can reach into the teens.

Black-headed caiques

CAIQUES

Region of Origin: South America

Group: Parrot

Size: 10 inches

Experience Level Needed by Owner: Some experience recommended

Price Range: About $1000

PHYSICAL FEATURES

Caiques (pronounced *ky-EEKS*) are mid-size parrots that have a short square tail. They have green backs, white stomachs, and yellow necks. In the **white-bellied caique** (*Pionites leucogaster*), the yellow continues upward to cover the entire head. In the **black-headed caique** (*Pionites melanocephala*), the yellow turns into a black cap. Both caique species are excellent compromises if you yearn for one of the large parrots, but decide that such a demanding bird requires too much time, space, and commitment.

ENERGETIC AND MISCHIEVOUS

The intelligent caique is curious and energetic. This combination can get him into mischief—caiques will figure their way out of their cage, and once these clever birds are out, they'll destroy everything in sight. They love to chew and should be supplied with plenty of nontoxic wooden toys. They like to shred cardboard boxes and play hide-and-seek in nest boxes and under newspapers, so provide these, as well.

Caiques are acrobatic clowns who enjoy doing comical tricks. They will roll and tumble in your hand. Many develop the odd habit of sleeping on their backs—they look quite dead until suddenly they scramble up to greet you! Because they are high-energy birds who have to be doing something most of the time, they may develop the habit of nipping at you while you're holding them. Provide caiques with a toy to nibble on while they're on your hand; this gives them a substitute for your fingers!

NOISY WHISTLERS

Caiques can be noisy with their shrill whistling calls. Many will wolf-whistle, and some will mimic, but in a small parrot voice.

YOUNG CAIQUES ONLY!

Black-headed caique

In the wild, caiques live deep in the forest and rarely approach human habitation, so imports, especially older ones, are quite wild. They seldom settle down and their powerful beak can deliver a hard bite. Purchase a young domestic hand-fed, if you can find one, and keep him as a single pet. This is especially important if your caique will be handled by children.

CANARY

Region of Origin: Canary Islands, off the coast of Africa

Group: Songbird

Size: 5 to 8 inches

Experience Level Needed by Owner: Fine for the novice

Price Range: $50 to $60

PHYSICAL FEATURES

The wild canary (*Serinus canaria*) is actually green, not yellow. He is so plain-looking that it's utterly amazing how he has been developed into the variety of breeds and colors that we have to choose from. The four groups of canaries discussed here have many distinct characteristics.

SONG CANARIES

These are canaries bred especially for their rich, melodious song. In the 1800s, song canaries were featured at grand balls, where they would sing a welcome as the guests arrived. Although some song canaries come in pretty colors, most do not have the most beautiful plumage. When exhibited at shows, they are not judged on what they look like, only on how perfectly they perform a particular singing pattern of "bubbles, rolls, and trills."

Trained song canaries are magnificent to hear. Some sing with their beak nearly closed, while others sing stretched up on their toes with their beak wide open. Even without training, song canaries sing beautifully.

The most popular and easiest-to-find song canaries are the **roller** and the **American singer.** The song of the roller is deep, mellow, and lulling, and tends to follow a predictable pattern. That of the American singer is more energetic and enthusiastic; he often makes it up as he goes along. American singers make especially good pets: they are steady, spirited birds who don't mind a lot of activity going on around them.

Note that only male canaries sing. Female canaries may warble softly, but they seldom sing.

TYPE (OR POSTURE) CANARIES

These canaries are bred for a specific type of appearance or posture. They must be a certain size, a certain color, with a head and tail shaped just so. Some breeds have been around for centuries and are still going strong, while others were once popular, but today are nearly extinct. New canary breeds are being developed all the time.

One of the most popular type canaries is the **border,** from the border between England and Scotland. This delightful canary is small, handsome, and lively. He comes in a variety of solid and mixed colors, including green, fawn, and blue. The **Fife canary** is an even smaller version of the border.

If you're looking for an unusual shape, the **Norwich** is large and stocky, while the **Yorkshire** is just the opposite: long, slim, and tapering. The elegant Yorkshire has been called "the gentleman of the fancy."

If you prefer a more unusual color, the **lizard** canary is the oldest known breed now in existence. His unusual speckled plumage is patterned like the scales of a lizard. Your guests will be scratching their heads trying to figure out just what kind of odd bird you've stumbled upon here!

If you'd like something even more unusual, the **Gloster** comes in crested and plain-headed varieties. A crested Gloster wears a cap of frilled hair that looks like a tiny string mop! Both crested and plain-headed birds are important in the Gloster breeding program because the two varieties must be paired for breeding; two cresteds produce odd-looking, sickly offspring, so each is needed to balance the other.

But the oddest canary of all is the **frilled.** Most of his plumage is long, silky, and wavy, while his thighs and breast are naked. Because of the complicated genetics involved, only experienced breeders can successfully produce these strange-looking, often nervous canaries.

Male posture canaries will sing, although not as beautifully as male song canaries.

COLOR-FACTOR CANARIES

These canaries are bred in over fifty colors, including red, orange, bronze, white, cinnamon, and something called silver agate opal. However, color-factor canaries hold their color only until they molt each year. When the colored feathers fall out, the new ones that grow in will not be colored unless you have carefully fed them a special "color food" throughout the molt. For example, without color feeding, red-factor canaries become pale orange or yellow after each molt.

If you're intrigued by the idea of changing the color of your pet canary from yellow to bright red, forget it. Color feeding cannot produce color in canaries who don't have genes for that color factor. In other words, the color must already be present in the canary for a color food to have any effect.

Male color-factor canaries will sing, but the song is sometimes shrill or harsh.

Pet-Shop Canaries

If you're hoping to stroll into your local pet shop and pick up a melodious roller canary or speckled lizard, you'll probably be out of luck. Although some pet shops have color-factor canaries, most offer only a general yellow canary (a "kitchen" canary) who is neither a song nor posture canary. But males will still sing, some more enthusiastically than others.

Our Oldest Songbird

The canary is the oldest caged songbird we know. For centuries, he was the most popular pet bird, but today the budgie has overtaken him. This is partly because the budgie will talk and perform tricks and is a more interactive bird, while the canary is not.

However, it is also partly because the budgie is "tougher" than the canary, which unfortunately means that he can withstand neglect for a longer period of time. Since so many prospective owners purchase birds on impulse, without knowing how to care for them, they are naturally looking for the "toughest" and "easiest" birds. This switch in popularity is a good thing for the canary, but not for the poor budgie.

The Gentle Canary

Canaries are lively and mild-mannered. Some are cheerful and curious about the world, while others are sweet and gentle, but a bit timid. Canaries usually will not entertain you with tricks, but their natural behaviors are amusing and fun to watch. Hand-raised canaries are friendly and can sometimes be finger-tamed, but most canaries are birds to observe and listen to, not to handle or play with.

If you've been reading about all the potential behavior problems of parrots, you'll be pleased to hear that the biggest behavior problem of canaries may be their habit of throwing seed hulls out of their cage!

THREE SEASONS OF SONG!

Canaries are songbirds, not mimics. Their voice is a soft, pleasant mixture of chirps and twitters. From October through May, males sing a lovely song; you'll feel like it's spring for three full seasons! During the molting months of June through September, they normally stop singing.

However, males may also stop singing if their feeding and housing requirements are not met. To sing happily, canaries require a varied diet, including greenery and calcium. They also require a roomy cage all to themselves; males usually won't sing when housed with another bird. The cage should be placed in a cool location—canaries don't like excessive heat—with good lighting. You should provide plenty of talking and whistling encouragement to keep them singing.

SINGLE CANARIES ARE FINE

The canary is the only common songbird who does well in a cage by himself. Canaries are sociable, though, so they do require human companionship. If you're away a lot, a canary may not be a good choice for you. If you want a singing canary, a single male in a roomy cage with sufficient human companionship is your best choice. You can add a female or even a pair of finches for companionship, but that usually causes the male to stop singing.

HEALTH PROBLEMS

Canaries have a reputation for being sickly, delicate, and short-lived, but that's because they are usually purchased by unknowledgeable owners, kept in tiny cages, and fed only seed. Canaries will live seven to fifteen years when properly cared for. They should be housed in a horizontal cage at least eighteen inches long, with two perches placed far apart to encourage flying. Most canaries don't play with toys, so don't clutter their flying room with toys meant for budgies.

Canaries should be fed a canary seed mix and a vitamin-rich conditioning food. Add cuttlebone and supplement with green vegetables such as romaine lettuce. Do not place them near drafts, do not frighten them, and handle them as little as possible; canaries are easily stressed and made ill by these three situations.

If you keep your bird in this way, you can congratulate yourself for being a responsible and knowledgeable canary owner. Instead of finding a dead bird on the bottom of your cage in a year or two, you will be rewarded with a decade or more of lovely plumage, enthusiastic activity, and beautiful singing.

Buy in Autumn

Since canaries breed in the spring, the best time to look for a young canary is in late fall, when the birds are between six months and one year old. Their first molt will be complete and the young canaries will be in full plumage. Males will be in full song. Prices will be reasonable because so many canaries are available.

If you want to buy a younger bird, it will be harder to distinguish males from females, although males often start to sing at about two months old. In behavior, males tend to be "prouder" than females; they hop boldly from perch to perch to "strut their stuff." Females are generally quieter and not as demonstrative.

In General

Though song canaries are bred for superior singing ability, that doesn't mean the other types don't sing. All male canaries, regardless of color or breed, can sing. The type of song does vary, however, and since everyone's taste is different, it's very important that you hear the song before taking your bird home. This is called "auditioning" your prospective bird.

If for some reason you can't audition a canary, insist upon a written guarantee that your bird is a male and will sing within two weeks, or you can bring "her" back.

COCKATIEL

Region of Origin: Australia

Group: Parrot

Size: 12 inches

Experience Level Needed by Owner: Fine for the novice

Price Range: $40 (normal grays) to $100 (fancier colors)

PHYSICAL FEATURES

The cockatiel (*Nymphicus hollandicus*), pronounced COCK-*a-teel,* is a small relative of the cockatoo, with broad powdery feathers and a pretty little head crest that can be raised and lowered. Unlike cockatoos, cockatiels come in a variety of colors, from silver to yellow. Among parrots, cockatiels are second only to budgies in popularity.

IDEAL BEGINNER'S BIRD

The cockatiel is an almost perfect beginner's bird: easily tamed and easily kept, with a gentle, friendly personality. He is peaceful with all the world and can be kept with other cockatiels or mixed with budgies. But as long as you're home enough, cockatiels don't need the companionship of another bird; they become so devoted to you that they will follow you around like a dog. They seem particularly entranced by human toes!

This delightful bird makes an ideal stepping-stone from budgies to the larger parrots. Or if you love cockatoos but can't afford one or can't provide all the time and attention they demand, the inexpensive and undemanding cockatiel is an excellent compromise. Adaptable to busy lifestyles and working owners, cockatiels make wonderful pets without the time requirements and behavioral problems of the larger parrots.

Cockatiels are sweet, lovable birds. Some are so affectionate they enjoy being cuddled and will solicit this attention, especially stroking on their cheek or behind their crest. Some cockatiels, however, don't particularly like being petted, although they can still be tame.

Also note that tame cockatiels often become one-person birds at maturity. They adore their special person, but may not tolerate handling by anyone else. Many cockatiels are great entertainers who perform acrobatic tricks. Like budgies, cockatiels often sit happily with their heads stuck up inside a clapper bell—no one knows why.

No bird is perfect, though. Cockatiels are fascinated by anything that gleams or glitters; they are forever filching bits of aluminum foil, coins, or jewelry, all of which are dangerous. They will chew, so supervision is essential when they are out of their cage or on their playground.

The sociable cockatiel should not be confined to a cage all the time, no matter how roomy. And the cage must be roomy, because cockatiels are strong fliers accustomed to open spaces. Although they are not hyperactive—when they're not playing, cockatiels sit placidly and observe the world—they do need plenty of room to flap their wings. The cage should be one and one-half to two feet in all three dimensions. Unfortunately, you'll find that many so-called cockatiel cages in pet shops are much too small.

NIGHT FRIGHTS

Another important reason to splurge for a large cage is that cockatiels are prone to an odd behavior called "night fright." In the middle of the night, a cockatiel may be sleeping peacefully when suddenly he begins thrashing in his cage, flapping his wings wildly and beating them against the bars. When this happens, he may break a wing feather and bleed profusely, which can endanger his life.

What causes night frights? Wild cockatiels are extremely alert and quick to fly at the slightest danger, so perhaps as pets they think they see or hear something frightening. Perhaps your dog rolled over in his sleep or your neighbor slammed his car door, or maybe your cockatiel simply bumped against a hanging toy in his cage. Birds don't see well in the dark.

To avoid night frights, provide a cage large enough to give your cockatiel room to flap. Don't hang toys close to his favorite sleeping perch. Leave a night light on so he can see where he's going should he suddenly panic. Some dedicated owners even purchase an inexpensive baby-monitor intercom system so they will be alerted should their cockatiel begin to thrash.

A GOOD CHOICE FOR CHILDREN

Because they are more docile and easier to handle than budgies, cockatiels make excellent parrots for children. They are highly recommended as anyone's first parrot.

DUSTY BIRDS

Besides their attractive little crest and pretty colors, a distinctive physical feature of cockatiels is their powdery feathers. All cockatiels have special down feathers that disintegrate into fine white dust. This natural feature helps absorb dust and dirt that could hinder flying, but unfortunately it's a nuisance in pet cockatiels.

When your cockatiel grooms himself, the powder floats through the air and lands on your floor and furniture. Some of it will come off on your hand when you pet him. Spraying your bird with a plant mister will help, but you must accept that cockatiels are dusty birds. Don't put their cages near bookshelves or computers. They are not good choices for a "neat-freak," or for an allergic or wheezy person.

COLORS

Once you've decided on a cockatiel, you'll be faced with a wide choice of colors (mutations) that have been developed from the normal wild cockatiel.

The normal cockatiel color is gray, with a yellow head and orange cheek patches. The cinnamon mutation is light brownish or cafe au lait. Lutino is a lovely suffusion of yellow and white. (Lutinos often have a bald spot on the back of their head; this isn't appreciated by breeders, but it's common nonetheless.) The pied is an intriguing mixture of patched colors. The whiteface lacks the yellow head markings.

The pearl mutation is very interesting, with silvery scalloped feathers that are absolutely lovely. Unfortunately, if your pearl cockatiel happens to be a male, he will lose those pearl markings at his first molt (about six months old) and look like a normal gray for the rest of his life. Pearl females, though, keep their coloring. Quite fascinating!

Double or triple mutations, such as pearl pied or whitefaced cinnamon pied, are gorgeous, but a real challenge to breed.

You might see a cockatiel advertised as "split" for a certain color. This means simply that the bird looks like a certain color and has one gene for that color, but also has a hidden gene for another color. This hidden color gene might show up in his offspring. This is essential knowledge for breeders, but of little use to pet owners. Split birds make the same kind of pet as any other cockatiel.

DOES COLOR AFFECT TEMPERAMENT?

This is the same question debated by budgie and lovebird fanciers. Some fanciers feel that the newer color mutations are smaller and sometimes not as stable and/or hardy as the normal or original colors.

This position has logic behind it, since breeding for new colors means that your choice of parents is limited. You must stick to those birds who can produce the specific colors you want, and sometimes temperament and behavior are given a back seat to color, at least until the color is well-established.

So you might find that the newer mutations are more high-strung and/or do not live quite as long as the grays and more established mutations. Lutinos, pieds, pearls, and whitefaces are more prone to night frights than grays and cinnamons.

TALKING ABILITY

Some cockatiels will mimic, but their vocabularies are limited and their voices are high-pitched and not especially clear. Males are louder and more vocal, so they make the best talkers. But if your chief interest is a talking bird, don't buy a cockatiel—their forte is personality, not mimicking.

Cockatiels are superior chirpers and whistlers, however. They will whistle an attractive greeting when you enter the room, and then a pleading entreaty not to leave! Their whistling is seldom loud enough to disturb the neighbors, although some adult males may whistle excessively in a shrill or screechy voice. These same male cockatiels will often memorize and mimic entire song verses.

ANY OTHER DIFFERENCES BETWEEN MALES AND FEMALES?

Yes, quite a few. Cockatiels are especially prone to temperament changes during the breeding season. Some handle their increased hormonal levels with few problems, but others become restless, hyperactive, or demanding. Many owners of sweet, affectionate cockatiels have been astounded and upset when their wonderful pet turns into a hissing tyrant between one and two years of age.

Males are the worst offenders. They often become nippy, strutting in front of mirrors and trying to breed everything in sight. Take away their mirrors and keep handling to a minimum during these cycles. Females are also more difficult during breeding seasons, but it's easier to discourage their flirtatious behaviors.

In general, male cockatiels are bolder and noisier, while females are more affectionate and often more acrobatic. However, there are exceptions; some males are quiet and gentle, while some females are independent or clownish.

If you buy a cockatiel at least six months old, it's easy to choose the sex you want. The yellow and orange head of the male is much brighter than that of the female, and the underside of his tail is solid, while the underside of hers is barred. If you want to be sure of a particular sex, don't be concerned about choosing a six-month-old cockatiel. Unlike most other parrots of similar size, older cockatiels are not very difficult to tame, especially if they've been hand-fed.

However, you may decide to take the surest taming route and buy an eight- to twelve-week-old hand-fed, just as you would with any other parrot. Young cockatiels have pinkish or light gray bills. They may have quill feathers sticking up on top of their head, giving them a comical appearance. Look for big round eyes, an alert posture, and a sweet (not hyperactive) temperament. Their feathers should have a slight talcum-powder feel from their powdery down.

Unfortunately, here's where you run into trouble with sexing. Until that first molt at about six months old, all young cockatiels look like females. So if you have your heart set on a young baby *and* a particular sex, be doubly sure to buy from only an experienced breeder; sometimes they can differentiate sex by behavior. Young males may have begun to whistle sharply or display other typically male activities such as bobbing their heads, squaring their shoulders, and hopping a lot.

When you're dealing with some of the color mutations, experienced breeders who know genetics can also predict sex, because some mutation colors are sex-linked. That means that a W-colored father bred to an X-colored mother will always produce Y-colored babies who are male and Z-colored babies who are female. The breeder will be able to tell the sex by the color.

In General

Cockatiels are hardy birds who do not need regular checkups or shots. You can expect to enjoy your cockatiel for fifteen to twenty-five years.

Citron cockatoo

COCKATOOS

Region of Origin: Indonesia and Australia

Group: Parrot

Size: 12 to 20 inches

Experience Level Needed by Owner: Experience recommended

Price Range: $500 to $2000 (see last paragraph of profile)

PHYSICAL FEATURES

Cockatoos are stout, majestic-looking birds with short broad tails. They have unusually broad feathers that make them seem larger than they really are. They are white or salmon pink, with yellow trim and a magnificent head crest that can be raised and spread like a fan. Cockatoos lift their wings, puff their feathers, and display their crest when they are excited or afraid, or to impress or intimidate another bird, a predator, or a human being. The large dark eye of the cockatoo moves freely in all directions, without his head needing to move—this is sometimes unnerving to people unfamiliar with these birds!

POWDERY BIRDS

Like cockatiels, cockatoos have down feathers that disintegrate into fine white powder. When the cockatoo grooms himself, the powder floats onto your floor, furniture, and bookcases. When you pet him, it comes off on your hand. Spraying the bird with a plant mister will help keep the powder contained, but you simply must accept that cockatoos are dusty birds. They are not good choices for a "neat-freak," or for an allergic or wheezy person.

EXTREMELY INTELLIGENT

The cockatoo is living proof that intelligence is not equated with speaking ability, because cockatoos may be the most intelligent of all parrots, even though their talking ability is not outstanding. Instead, the intelligence of the cockatoo takes the form of intense curiosity and an aptitude for activities that require great dexterity. Most cockatoos display uncanny levels of understanding, ingenuity, and abstract reasoning.

Cockatoos are proud birds, keenly aware of their surroundings and quick to display their wings and crests to an admirer. If the admirer should fail to notice and appreciate this boastful display, a loud demanding scream is sure to attract attention!

EXTREMELY EMOTIONAL AND AFFECTIONATE

Along with being among the most intelligent parrots, cockatoos are the most emotional and affectionate parrots as well. Indeed, their emotional make-up is quite humanlike, running the gamut from deep devotion and delightfully or mischievously humorous, to jealousy and even temper tantrums.

These demonstrative birds are wonderful cuddlers who thrive on caressing and stroking. It has been said that cockatoos would like to be surgically attached to their owner. On the surface, this sounds so wonderful that the cockatoo is on practically everybody's wish list at one time or another, but the intense craving for affection and attention can create a host of problems for unprepared owners.

Cockatoos are so devoted that they often choose their owner as their "mate." During breeding season, they will make flirtatious courtship gestures toward you, and they may sulk or bite when you laughingly push them away.

EXTREMELY NOISY!

Like the other large parrots, cockatoos utter blood-curdling screams once or twice each day, just for the sheer love of making noise. And if you thought Amazons and macaws were loud, just wait until you hear a cockatoo shriek. This daily screeching usually occurs at sunrise and sunset, which would be the typical feeding times in the wild. The shrieking is sometimes called their "happy cockatoo routine" by their fond—and exasperated!—owners.

Cockatoos also throw ear-splitting tantrums if neglected or thwarted. If you yell back at them, you will only prolong their screaming. Obviously, these are not apartment birds.

Suitable Owner for a Cockatoo

The vast majority of prospective bird owners should not even consider a cockatoo because these fabulous birds are the most demanding of all parrots. They think the world revolves around them, and they can be stubborn and upset when they don't get their way. Cockatoos must have owners with predictable schedules, who are prepared to devote enormous amounts of time and effort in making the bird a full-fledged member of the family. These birds can be kept by families who are away much of the day if they've been trained as babies to amuse themselves with their toys. However, arrangements must be made to let them out of their cages several times a day. It's much, much better if someone is home all day or if you can take your cockatoo to work with you.

Cockatoos are a major commitment. These gregarious birds must be allowed to share and participate. Indeed, they insist upon giving and receiving attention, and the lengths they will go to achieve it are sometimes hilarious, sometimes annoying, and sometimes a real problem. If left alone for long periods of time and not given several hours of daily attention, cockatoos will shriek themselves hoarse and pluck their feathers out.

Even when given plenty of attention cockatoos can be difficult to live with. They are chewers who should never be left unsupervised on an open perch, for they will climb down and destroy every wooden object in sight. Even when left in a locked cage, they are escape artists—many owners padlock the cage!

Finally, although cockatoos are generally sweet and good-natured, and seldom are bad biters, their emotional states can be hard to keep up with. Some individuals switch rapidly among extreme cuddliness, mischievousness, and sulkiness.

Discipline

Cockatoos have a reputation for being "naturally" tame, affectionate, and cuddly, but many new owners have discovered, to their dismay, that this is not true. Besides daily time and attention, cockatoos need discipline. They must be taught to respond to commands such as "Up" and "Down."

If you feel you may be intimidated by these big birds, you should not buy one. A spoiled baby cockatoo will become a spoiled adult cockatoo, and you'll end up with screaming and feather-plucking when the bird doesn't get his own way. So when you bring your baby home, don't constantly play with him or pick him up every time you walk by his cage. He is so intelligent that he'll come to expect you to pick him up every time you walk by his cage and will throw a fit when you don't.

DOMESTIC VERSUS IMPORTED

As with most parrots, there is an enormous difference between imported cockatoos and hand-fed cockatoos. Hand-feds are inquisitive and trusting, retaining their adorable baby traits for a long time. Cockatoos are notoriously difficult to wean, so novice owners should never purchase a baby cockatoo who is still hand-feeding. Buy him only after he is fully weaned, usually at about four months.

In stark contrast, training imports to overcome their timidity takes a great deal of time, effort, and patience. Many imports never gain full confidence in humans.

NOT OUTSTANDING TALKERS

Cockatoos are capable of accurate sound effects, easily mimicking a refrigerator motor or a ringing telephone. However, few cockatoos are skilled at mimicking human speech. Some individuals develop decent vocabularies, but their voices are parrotlike and often harsh. If you want a talking bird, a cockatoo is not for you.

ENTERTAINING TRICKS

Many cockatoos are great entertainers, performing acrobatic stunts such as roller-skating, riding a bike, or walking a tightrope. Unlike some other parrots, such as Amazons, the intelligent and devoted cockatoo works for affection and praise more than for food.

MALE OR FEMALE?

In general, male cockatoos are considered easier to tame, but it's difficult if not impossible to sex cockatoos by appearance.

Roomy Cage

Since cockatoos are lively and acrobatic, their cage must be roomy, about four feet wide by two feet deep by four feet high. They should be provided with tree branches to chew on, and a variety of chewable toys, rotated to maintain interest. The cage must be strong and secure, preferably padlocked, or these clever escape artists will pop the welds with their powerful beaks, or even open the latch. Once they are out, they will wreak havoc in your house.

However, this doesn't mean that the padlock should stay on all the time. Cockatoos must be allowed some free time on a playground or bird tree. But they require supervision during their playtime because they are quick to climb down and explore your house.

Health Problems

Cockatoos are very susceptible to psittacine beak and feather syndrome (PBFS), so much so that it is often called cockatoo disease. This devastating disease is discussed more fully in Chapter 10. Make sure the baby you are looking at has had health cultures done by an avian vet, and make sure there is good powder on the feathers.

Cockatoos can be picky eaters and are susceptible to malnutrition-related illnesses. It's important to feed a nutritious pellet diet supplemented with lots of grains, fruits, and vegetables.

In General

Cockatoos are long-lived parrots. You must be positive that you want to live with the emotional equivalent of a two-year-old child for fifty years.

Also, cockatoos are not for busy people, since these are the worst of all birds to neglect. Nor are cockatoos for the faint-hearted, so if you are looking for a docile, subdued little birdie to sit quietly in a small cage, a cockatoo is not for you. If, on the other hand, you have lots of time to devote to a bird of breathtaking beauty and fantastic personality, a cockatoo makes one of the most satisfying pets of all the big parrots.

Ten species of cockatoo are commonly available as pets. The first two are native to the Moluccan Islands of Indonesia.

Moluccan cockatoo (*Cacatua moluccensis*)

One of the largest of the cockatoos at twenty inches, the Moluccan is powerful and majestic. His white body is delicately suffused with pink, and his pinkish-red crest provides the alternate name of salmon-crested cockatoo.

In the past, Moluccans were commonly imported, but the wild population has been drastically depleted by habitat destruction. Moluccans are considered an endangered species and may no longer be imported. However, smugglers still bring in illegal birds, usually in poor health and with unstable temperaments. You need to be very careful when buying a Moluccan; stick with the domestic hand-feds, who are cuddly and easy to tame.

Moluccans are harder to generalize about than some of the other cockatoos—they have complex, variable personalities and no two are alike. They are usually considered the most outgoing, high-spirited, and entertaining cockatoos. They love to perform and show off for admiration and praise, requiring very roomy cages with lots of toys.

They are also some of the most affectionate, sensitive, and emotional of cockatoos. This can be good or bad, depending upon how much time you have available for them and the degree of care you give. Moluccans are extremely demanding and often become overzealous in seeking your attention. Unless you are a firm owner who can stick to rules, Moluccans are prone to temper tantrums and other behavioral problems when they don't get their way. Some will deliberately throw food and other unwanted items out of their cage.

Moluccans are also extremely vocal; some will learn to talk and whistle, but most are content with chattering and screaming.

If you're a big-hearted animal lover looking for an "abused" cockatoo to rehabilitate, Moluccans are not a good choice. Abused or neglected Moluccans develop serious, deep-seated problems, and it takes a very long time to win their trust and change their behavior. This demanding task is best left to experienced bird owners.

Umbrella cockatoo (*Cacatua alba*)

Not quite as large as the Moluccan at seventeen inches, the umbrella or great white cockatoo has snowy white plumage, including his wide full crest. Umbrellas are commonly (and legally) imported from the Moluccan Islands, but they are such good breeders in captivity that plenty of hand-fed babies are available, and should be your only choice as a pet.

The umbrella is a very popular cockatoo, and rightfully so. He is exceptionally gentle and easy to tame, the most cuddly and affectionate of all cockatoos. His only drawback may be that, like the Moluccan, his great devotion makes him crave constant attention, often making excessive demands on his owner's time. Similarly, most umbrellas are very emotional, sensitive, and sometimes high-strung. They have loud, chattering voices, but they seldom use them for talking.

The remaining cockatoos are native to Australia. Australian cockatoos are often considered more emotionally stable than those from the Moluccan Islands, but they are also not as cuddly. Australian cockatoos are mostly white with a yellow (or orange) crest and a light yellow suffusion on their cheeks and underparts.

Greater sulphur-crested cockatoo (*Cacatua galerita galerita*)

This twenty-inch giant has a tremendous wingspread and requires plenty of room. The greater sulphur-crested is a hardy bird, quick to learn and very talented, but he definitely knows his own mind and has too strong a personality for a novice owner.

Triton cockatoo (*Cacatua galerita triton*)

At eighteen inches, the triton can be distinguished from the greater sulphur-crested by his blue eye ring. This is one of most trainable cockatoos, as evidenced by the talented Fred who charmed audiences on the TV show "Baretta." Some tritons will talk a little, although their voice is typical cockatoo—rather harsh. If you like your cockatoos big, the triton is less strong-willed than the greater sulphur-crested and makes a more practical pet.

Eleanora cockatoo (*Cacatua galerita eleanora*)

If the triton is still too large for you, the eleanora is fifteen inches, with a white eye ring. Not as easy to find as some of the others, he is still a popular pet, with all of the typical cockatoo characteristics.

Lesser sulphur-crested cockatoo (*Cacatua sulphurea*)

Coming down still further in size, the thirteen-inch lesser is suited to smaller homes. He is less outgoing than his larger cousins and doesn't speak well or do many tricks, but he is also less demanding of attention and less noisy. Some are a bit shy or independent, but others make affectionate, trustworthy pets.

Citron cockatoo (*Cacatua citrinocristata*)

Similar in size to the lesser sulphur-crested, the citron is easily distinguished by his orange crest. Many citrons are outgoing and gregarious—in fact, some are real hams.

Goffin's cockatoo (*Cacatua goffini*)

The Goffin is white with pinkish-red feathers scattered around his eyes and forehead. His short white crest forms a spike or horn in the middle of his crown.

Most cockatoos are alert and curious, but the Goffin is even more so. This comical ham is lively and playful. His beak may not be very large, but this clever bird knows exactly how to use it to pick the latch on his cage. The Goffin grows and develops more slowly than other cockatoos and lives a very long time. Some develop fair vocabularies.

The Goffin is the least expensive cockatoo, but too many people jump blindly at those low prices, thinking they're bringing home that "winning, cuddly cockatoo personality." Low prices usually belong to the imported birds, and these are among the hardest of all cockatoos to tame. You may have to search for a domestic hand-fed, because the Goffin doesn't breed well in captivity, but you must resolve to be successful in your search and settle for nothing less.

Bare-eyed cockatoo (*Cacatua sanguinea*)

Also called the little corella, the bare-eyed cockatoo is not as striking in appearance as the others. He is mostly white with a barely noticeable crest and naked skin around his eyes. In personality, however, the bare-eyed stands out as perhaps the most intelligent of all cockatoos, and definitely the best talker. This outgoing species loves people. He is cheerful and friendly, with an affinity for clever games and comical tricks.

Rose-breasted cockatoo (*Eolophus roseicapillus*)

Called galah in Australia and considered as common as a pigeon (but ten times as pesty), the rose-breasted cockatoo is extremely expensive in the United States. His short, squat, rather ungraceful build *is* somewhat pigeonlike, and he does look very different from other cockatoos. His coloration is also different, but there is nothing ungraceful about it: a striking combination of rosy pink and gray that is absolutely gorgeous.

The rose-breasted cockatoo is highly intelligent and sweet-natured. He's more easygoing than other cockatoos and adapts well to family life. Although he's not much of a cuddler, he does love to interact with people by showing off and performing comical acrobatics. Because he is extremely busy and inquisitive, he's fun to watch as he runs around the floor of your house. These cockatoos prefer the ground to the air and are very curious, so make sure you've picked up your valuables and anything small that could be swallowed.

Many rose-breasteds will talk, although their speech is not very clear. A big plus is that they seldom raise their voice enough to be a nuisance. They sound somewhat like cockatiels. If you must have a cockatoo in an apartment, this one is probably your best bet.

Rose-breasted cockatoos can often become overweight and can develop fatty tumors. They should be fed pellets, grains, and fresh vegetables and fruits. No seeds should be included in their diet.

Some other cockatoo species are not readily available or adaptable to home life. The **Major Mitchell's leadbeater cockatoo** (*Cacatua leadbeateri*), with his splendidly colored crest like a feathered parfait, is considered the crown jewel of any cockatoo collection, but he is not a house pet. He can cost as much as a used car, and is extremely independent, noisy, and destructive; the leadbeater belongs only in experienced hands. The **black cockatoos** (several species of *Calyptorhynchus*) are also strikingly beautiful, but they are too rare and costly to be accessible to the general public.

WHAT WILL YOU PAY FOR YOUR COCKATOO?

As we've discussed, the Goffin is generally the most inexpensive cockatoo, starting at three hundred dollars and going up to six hundred; you should happily pay the higher price for a hand-fed. Umbrellas, citrons, lesser sulphur-cresteds, eleanoras, and bare-eyeds run between five hundred and one thousand dollars. Moluccans and tritons start at twelve hundred, while greater sulphur-cresteds and rose-breasteds start at eighteen hundred.

Green-cheeked conure

CONURES

Region of Origin: Central and South America, and Mexico

Group: Parrot

Size: 10 to 13 inches

Experience Level Needed by Owner: Some experience recommended

Price Range: Most common species are less than $200

PHYSICAL FEATURES

There are more than thirty species of conures, most of which are green with various head markings. A few species are more brilliantly colored.

CLEVER, DYNAMIC PARROTS IN A COMPACT BODY

Although conures are closer in size to Australian parakeets than to the bigger parrots, their temperament and behavior are more reminiscent of the latter. The clever conure is extremely active, bold, and curious. He will climb all over his cage (which should be two to three feet in all three dimensions), hang upside down and screech, and happily chew up his toys. Outside of his cage, he is mischievous and destructive—nothing is safe from his strong, inquisitive beak.

Conures are not soothing pets, but if you like parrots with strong and fearless personalities, and if you can put up with their energy level, they make delightfully spunky pets. They must be acquired as young hand-feds, though, because older conures resist taming and can deliver a nasty bite. Even hand-feds are nippy if you push them too far. If you want to handle your conure, be sure to keep his wings clipped; it will calm him down.

Conures are like caiques: these high-energy birds have to be doing something all the time. If they nip while you're holding them, try giving them a toy to nibble on while they're on your hand—this gives them a substitute for your fingers.

Conures are also similar to caiques in their enjoyment of nontoxic wooden toys, cardboard boxes to shred, nest boxes and newspapers, so provide these as well. They may also roll over and sleep on their backs, which can be a shocking sight if you're not expecting it!

NOISY, NOISY, NOISY!

As a group, conures are considered among the noisiest screechers of all parrots. Though single conures are quieter than a whole group of them, and while hand-feds usually restrict their screaming to times when they want attention, that's little solace if you prefer a quiet household. Most conures are not good talkers, and of those that are, their vocabularies are small and their voices loud and unpleasant. Still, conures who have learned to talk often substitute human words for screeching—that's something worth considering!

MALE OR FEMALE?

Neither appearance nor behavior distinguishes the sexes. In fact, even the various species of conure are often hard to distinguish.

IN GENERAL

Conures are hardy birds who can live fifteen to thirty years. You can purchase most common species for under two hundred dollars, but the strikingly beautiful sun and jenday conures, along with the large Patagonian conure, can cost over four hundred dollars. With so many species available, don't feel restricted to the ones listed here. If you're interested in the general conure profile, feel free to give all conures a serious look.

Maroon-bellied conure (also called red-bellied)
(*Pyrrhura frontalis*)

The maroon-bellied is the quietest conure; mostly he just makes a clacking sound, although even that may not be pleasant to listen to. Sometimes he'll mimic a few words. He is attractive in a simple way: green with a maroon forehead and stomach patch. Young maroon-bellieds are easily tamed, friendly, and comical. Like all conures, the inquisitiveness of the maroon-bellied may maneuver him out of his cage to chew up your woodwork. This species is readily available for about a hundred dollars, so if you're interested in a conure, you should put the maroon-bellied high on your list, along with a similar conure from the *Pyrrhura* genus, the **green-cheeked** (*P. molinae*).

Half-moon conure (also called orange-fronted)
(*Aratinga canicularis*)

This green conure takes his name from the orange crescent on his forehead. Some young half-moons are easily tamed and make delightful pets, while others seem to resist taming. Some will learn to mimic a few words.

Peach-fronted conure (also called golden-crowned)
(*Aratinga aurea*)

The peach-fronted has an orange marking on his forehead, but can be distinguished from the half-moon by his beak color. The peach-fronted has a solid black beak, while the half-moon has a horn-colored beak. The peach-fronted will sometimes mimic words and sounds, and is a deservedly popular pet. He's a typical conure, though—lively and loud.

Other Conures

A group of similar conures who share a red head include the **mitred** (*A. mitrata*), the **white-eyed** (*A. leucopthalmus*), and **cherryhead** (*A. erythrogenys*). Even more than other conures, this group is boisterous, loud, and often nippy. But it is also acrobatic and affectionate, and the birds often make good talkers. If your personality can handle the bad with the good, these dynamic conures make fun-loving clowns.

If you're interested in the largest conure, you might look at the lovely **Patagonian** (*Cyanoliseus patagonus*). This eighteen-inch bird has a long tapering tail that must be considered when arranging housing. He is highly intelligent, adores stroking and cuddling, and may mimic a few words in a clear, high-pitched voice. However, his bloodcurdling shrieks will not make you a welcome neighbor in close quarters.

The **sun conure** (*Aratinga solstitialis*) and the related **jenday** (*Aratinga jandaya*) are a striking combination of golden yellow, deep orange, and greenish blue. Young hand-feds are very playful and clownish. Their biggest drawback is that they are painfully noisy, and I don't mean talking. Jendays especially have very loud, piercing voices and love to shriek.

Finally, there's a conure who is not the best choice for the average household. The **nanday conure** (*Nandayus nenday*) is greenish with a black head and tail. Hand-feds sometimes make good pets, but nandays are often nippy and exceedingly noisy. Their excruciating screams and raucous calls will split your eardrums and have all your neighbors lining up at your door with justifiable complaints. Unless you live in the boonies, pass on this one.

Jenday conure

ECLECTUS

Region of Origin: South Pacific islands and Australia

Group: Parrot

Size: 15 inches

Experience Level Needed by Owner: Some experience recommended

Price Range: Over $1000

PHYSICAL FEATURES

The eclectus is one of the few parrots in which the sexes are easily distinguished by appearance. You have only two color choices: one for males and one for females.

But what exquisite color choices they are!

Male eclectus parrots are vibrant green, while female eclectus are vivid red-and-blue. This extreme sexual differentiation is so unusual among parrots that aviculturists once thought the males and females were two different species. It is said that eclectus were once worshipped as sacred birds because of their gaudy colors. The texture of eclectus feathering is unusual, too: so glossy and silky that it resembles mammal hair.

MILD-MANNERED PARROTS

Eclectus are gentle and mild-mannered, somewhat shyer than other parrots in their size range. When they feel at home, they are playful, friendly, and easy to tame. In an unfamiliar situation they may freeze up, so they should always be handled calmly and confidently, which will in turn boost their confidence.

Eclectus love to climb and should be provided with a three-foot cage with sturdy tree branches so they can get plenty of exercise. They are not destructive, so they should be allowed some free playtime on a gym. If confined too much, they will become lethargic. Choose a young, hand-fed eclectus.

NOT TOO NOISY

Eclectus will chatter and chuckle, and many will mimic a few words, especially males. Some can even imitate specific voices, as well as the words. A friend of mine has a male eclectus who calls "Mom! Mom!" in an exact imitation of her daughter's voice. This same bird says, "Come back!" whenever I put my hand on the front door knob to leave. Unlike the larger parrots, eclectus do not usually engage in regular periods of screaming.

MALE OR FEMALE?

Males are gentler, easier to tame, and make the best talkers. Females are the more dominant show-offs, and some become bossy and nippy at maturity.

IN GENERAL

There are about a dozen subspecies of eclectus, including the grand (*Eclectus roratue roratus*), red-sided (*E. r. polychloros*), vosmaeri (*E. r. vosmaeri*), and Solomon Island (*E. r. solomonensis*). They are all similar in appearance and behavior.

Gouldian finches

FINCHES

Region of Origin: Australia, Africa, and Asia

Group: Songbird

Size: 4 to 6 inches

Experience Level Needed by Owner: Some species are fine for the novice, while some experience is recommended for other species

Price Range: Price varies from four dollars for a zebra finch to sixty dollars for a Gouldian finch. However, you're never purchasing only one finch at a time, so you need to multiply your cost by at least two, and preferably by four or six

PHYSICAL FEATURES

Finches often attract considerable attention because of their tiny size, lively antics, and funny *beep-beeps*. Finches are small, quick, and delicate, constantly flitting about, sitting in long rows touching the bird next to them, and twittering cheerfully. Many species with an assortment of colors and color combinations are available, which adds to the fun of choosing species.

ARE FINCHES FOR YOU?

Too many people purchase a single finch (or a random pair) and a tiny cage without enough thought for their special needs. If you want a playful bird that you can handle, a finch is not for you. Finches are not parakeets; they do not like to sit on your finger, they do not like to be petted, they don't talk, and they seldom play with toys. Finches are observation birds; when housed in a roomy cage in a quiet sun room, they make bright, lively pets.

If you want a single bird, a finch is also not for you. These sociable birds must not be kept alone or they will pine. At the very least, you should buy two birds who have already paired up and house them in a cage at least one and one-half feet in all three dimensions. Ideally, buy two or three pairs and house them in a cage four feet long by two feet deep by two feet high. Finches may be small, but they are very active and must have a long horizontal cage in which to fly. The general rule is to provide three square feet of floor space per pair.

Once you understand that thousands of finches die early from stress caused by handling, solitary confinement, and cramped living conditions, you may be ready for finches.

FINCH SONGS

Finches do not sing as melodiously as canaries. Their soft songs vary from flutelike trills to throaty warbles, but they're not very musical. The most reliable songsters are the singing finch and the European goldfinch. The zebra finch has a funny little song that sounds like a trumpet.

In most of the species discussed here, only the males sing to any great extent. Thus, listening to finches is often the best (sometimes the only) way to determine sex. Sometimes several finches will gather around a singing male and listen intently to him.

Besides singing or warbling, finches engage in a variety of twittering and chattering noises—and the noisiest finches tend to be the same ones who make good singers! Noisy, however, may be too harsh a term: three pairs of gossiping zebra finches are not going to disturb your neighbors.

MIX-AND-MATCH YOUR OWN
COLORFUL GROUP OF SONGBIRDS

Although finches have a reputation for gentleness, some species are aggressive toward each other. It is one of life's little ironies—or perhaps one of Murphy's laws—that the trouble-making finches tend to be the most beautiful species!

Problem finches include the cut-throat, parson, melba, crimson, and violet-eared waxbill, as well as several twinspots and firefinches—species not discussed here. (Interestingly, finches with blue or red markings are often aggressive toward other finches with blue or red markings.) Some of these finches are not only unsuitable in a mixed aviary but cannot be kept even in groups of their own kind because the males will fight. Only a single pair should be kept in a single cage. So if you want only two finches, you should certainly study up on these gorgeous birds.

However, if you're thinking of two or three pairs of finches in the same cage, or if you'd like to combine species, you should look at peaceful finches. These are species who will live comfortably with each other in a mixed group of males and females. They include the zebra, society, owl, cherry, painted, star, European goldfinch, singing finch, Gouldian, and most *Lonchura* finches (mannikins, munias, nuns, and silverbills).

If you'd like to mix finches with other kinds of birds, remember that finches are afraid of birds larger than themselves. Novices should mix finches only with gentle canaries. Finches should never be mixed with budgies (parakeets).

FASCINATING SOCIAL BEHAVIOR

A group of finches is fascinating to watch. They usually huddle together, leaning against each other and grooming each other. Some species sit in long rows and groom any bird they happen to be next to. Other species sit in pairs and groom the same bird all the time. Still others only groom other birds during the breeding season.

In a mixed aviary, you must provide several food and water dishes to reduce competition and bickering. You must also be on constant guard against bullies who pick fights over favorite perches and other silly things. Males and females make equally effective bullies; males won't hesitate to bite females and even young birds. Finches threaten each other by hissing and pecking.

You know you've got a bully in your aviary when one of your finches sits straight up, trying to make himself as slim and "invisible" as possible. Or he may hide in a corner and lay down his feathers as flat as possible. You must either remove this bird or the bully bird. If the situation is not remedied, the victim will eventually die of exhaustion or heart failure.

HOUSING

Finches come from warm climates, so they need warmth. They should be kept in a room at least sixty-eight degrees all year. Finches are not suitable for outdoor living in any climate where the temperature dips below freezing for even one night, else you will find them dead in the morning. They love the sun and enjoy the outdoors when it's over sixty degrees, but they require a heated indoor room the rest of the time. Some finches also like a wooden or wicker basket for sleeping, or they may catch cold or panic at the slightest disturbance. Nest sleepers include the zebra, society, owl, star finch, and some *Lonchuras*. To decorate the cage, natural branches and greenery are much preferred to plastic pet-shop furnishings.

BREEDING

Many people choose finches because they want the excitement of raising babies. Unless you are prepared to keep all of the young, be aware that it's not easy to find good homes for finches. Since the average household is not prepared to care properly for finches, you will need to screen homes carefully to find suitable environments.

Zebra and society finches have lived and bred in captivity for generations, so if you stick with these two, you can mix them in a large cage and they will happily build nests, lay eggs, and raise their young for you. Trying to breed other finches requires more knowledge, as they often require an aviary to breed. They may live happily in a roomy cage, but they won't breed there.

BUYING FINCHES

Because of their short life span (two to eight years), only finches under one year of age should be purchased. To be sure of the age, choose finches who wear metal—not plastic—bands around their leg. Metal bands can be put on only within a few weeks of birth, while plastic bands can be slipped on any time.

Australia prohibits the export of its wild birds, so all Australian finches have been bred in captivity. They are healthy and comfortable with our food and climate. In contrast, many African finches have been stressed from importation; do not buy wild-caught Africans.

When choosing finches, look for alertness and liveliness. Finches don't normally sleep during the day, so a napping or lethargic finch could be ill. Try to choose finches who have already paired up of their own accord, but if you're interested in breeding, be aware that "pairs" are sometimes of the same sex.

When they're first brought home, finches can be delicate and easily frightened, so they should be carefully introduced into their new environment. Don't allow any loud noises or sudden movements around them for the first few days.

Finches must be kept in good condition right from the beginning because it is difficult to nurse them back to health. They are very prone to colds and pneumonia, and drafts will kill these little birds.

The following profiles feature hardy species who eat simple foods, don't need huge aviaries, and are tolerant of imperfect care. When you make your inevitable mistakes—as we all do when first raising birds—these finches won't lose their lives because of them.

Zebra finch (*Taeniopygia guttata*)

The zebra finch is the perfect choice for novice finch owners. This perky, inquisitive little species is one of the hardiest of all finches, extremely easy to care for. He is a vigorous, sometimes hyperactive little bird, always in motion and amusing to watch. His persistent call of *bee-bee-bee-bee-bee* can become monotonous, but he also belts out an unusual trumpeting song. Zebras are very easy breeders—they are willing to breed in a cage as small as three feet long.

The normal zebra color is grayish, and his barred tail gives him his name. Males have orange cheek patches. There are many color mutations from which you can choose, including silver, fawn, cream, cinnamon, white, and pied. Every year new color variations are developed for these handsome finches. The zebra is an Australian finch.

Owl finch (*Stizoptera bichenovii*)

This tiny finch is named for his round white facial disk, similar to that of an owl. His personality is friendly and peaceful, lively and amusing. This gregarious species would make a wonderful addition to your community aviary. He is an Australian finch.

Cherry finch (*Aidemosyne modesta*)

The cherry gets his name from his purplish-red crown. This lovely and peaceful finch will not cause any problems in your community aviary. He is an Australian finch.

Painted finch (*Emblema pictum*)

The gorgeous painted finch is peaceful with other finches, and often friendly with people. His red face and tail stand out. He is an Australian finch.

Star finch (*Neochmia ruficauda*)

This olive finch has a bright red face. He is good-natured and peaceful and often has a nice little song. The star is an Australian finch.

European goldfinch (*Carduelis carduelis*)

The European goldfinch is a centuries-old species, extremely popular in Victorian Europe, especially in Great Britain. This attractive finch with bright golden yellow on his wings will be the sweet songster of your aviary, with a tinkling call note and a light song. He may not sing as frequently as a canary, but his song is often more cheerful. Males can be picked out by their singing and their larger red facial masks.

These goldfinches are hardy, friendly, and peaceful. They can be kept in pairs or groups and mixed with other finches. They do well when mixed with canaries, but they will interbreed with the canaries to produce hybrids. Because European goldfinches are extremely active and acrobatic, they need a roomy cage at least thirty inches long. Their diet should be supplemented with fruits, greens, and a seed mixture called song food, which contains dark oily seeds.

Society finch (*Lonchura domestica*)

The society finch, another ideal choice for the novice, is a perfect name for this gregarious little bird. He is friendly, peaceful, and very easy to care for. This finch has an interesting history; he is not found in the wild at all, but was created and bred entirely in captivity.

Society finches are the most reliable breeders of all. They would happily spend their entire lives raising their own young—and the young of other species. Society finches make superb foster parents. They are so sociable and

helpful that they often crowd together into one nest and share eggs! This can bring about stepped-on and broken eggs, so if you want a successful clutch, place each pair of society finches into its own cage for breeding.

The society finch is usually white with chocolate, chestnut, or fawn markings. The variations on this pied coloring means that no two look exactly alike. Unlike the zebra finch, the sex of society finches cannot be distinguished by appearance, so you'll have to listen for the male's squeaky little song.

Singing finch

This is the first African finch we've discussed, and since Africans are commonly imported, be sure you're looking at domestic-breds. You'll have a choice of the more colorful green (*Serinus mozambieus*) or the enthusiastic singing grey (*Serinus leucopygia*). The singing finch will be the other songster in your aviary, offering musical twitters and a soft canarylike song—males only, of course. Singing finches improve their performance by listening to the songs of other birds.

The hardy singing finch can live into his late teens and is lively, curious, and easy to care for. You should only keep one pair at a time—more will fight—but that pair can be mixed with other finches and canaries. Like the European goldfinch, though, the singing finch is happy to hybridize with the canaries.

Lonchura finches (mannikins, munias, nuns, silverbills)

If you want African or Asian finches who are peaceful, the members of the *Lonchura* genus are good choices for the novice. Make sure they are domestic-bred.

Mannikins, munias, nuns, and silverbills are hardy, undemanding finches who live a long time. These plain-looking birds don't have the most exciting or entertaining personalities, but they are pleasant and easy to care for. Most *Lonchuras* are peaceful and sociable, often visiting each other's nests and sitting together in a long line.

If you want a singing *Lonchura,* opt for the silverbill with his soft warbling song.

Gouldian finch (*Chloebia gouldiae*)

The final finch we discuss is perhaps the most gorgeous of all, sometimes called the Lady Gouldian. This strikingly beautiful finch was discovered in Australia by the great naturalist John Gould.

The Gouldian is a popular show bird who will add stunning color to your aviary. Each Gouldian is a brilliant combination of red, blue, green, yellow, and purple, with each color in its own sharply divided area. There are several color mutations, primarily in head color. Adults are easy to sex; the chest of the male is bright purple, while that of the female is mauve.

Gouldians are peaceful and mild-mannered, but they do have some very special needs. Because they come from the hottest parts of Australia, their cage must be kept at seventy degrees minimum, preferably closer to eighty degrees. Because they can become ill from too little exercise, their cage must be roomy and their perches placed far apart to encourage flying. Gouldians should be kept in good-sized groups, and unfortunately, they cost about sixty dollars apiece.

Gouldians are more delicate than the other finches we've discussed. It can be difficult to keep them healthy and thriving; some die suddenly for no apparent reason, while others are afflicted with odd illnesses. You should gain some experience with the easier finches before bringing the magnificent Gouldian into your home. You may be a well-meaning finch owner, but you don't want your inexperience or accidental neglect to lead to tragedy.

GREY-CHEEKED PARAKEET

Region of Origin: South and Central America

Group: Parrot

Size: 9 inches

Experience Level Needed by Owner: Fine for the novice

Price Range: About $100

PHYSICAL FEATURES

This small species (*Brotogeris pyrrhopterus*) is mostly green with light gray cheeks and a light blue crown. In his native lands, huge flocks of grey-cheeks destroy plantation crops. The natives use large nets to catch them and export them to the United States, where they become pets rather than pests.

CHEERFUL AND CURIOUS

Grey-cheeks are an excellent choice for those who like their birds bold, curious, and lively, but also small. Taming is easy, especially with young hand-feds, although these can be hard to find. Grey-cheeks don't breed readily in captivity, so most of those offered for sale are imports.

The grey-cheek is both smart and demanding. He likes companionship so much that he may crawl across your shoulders and poke his busy little head into your shirt pocket. This habit, combined with his small size, probably created his alternate name of pocket parrot. He is often called a bee bee parrot, as well.

As much as they enjoy climbing on *you,* grey-cheeks enjoy playing on bird gyms and playgrounds. They should be supervised, though, since they are prone to mischief outside their cage.

His main disadvantages are his tendency to become nippy and his harsh voice, which can drive you up the wall. Fortunately, single pets do not tend to be as noisy. Still, this feisty little bird will scold you when he is displeased and shriek when he is angry. Grey-cheeks love to be noticed, and they may learn to mimic if you shower them with attention when they do it. But if you *don't* shower them with attention, they won't hesitate to switch to ear-splitting whistles!

They will choose and reject toys with the same speak-their-mind attitude. One grey-cheek would examine a new toy and boldly state his opinion: "I hate it!" or "Cool!"

You can count on your hardy grey-cheek being part of your family for up to fifteen years.

A SIMILAR SPECIES

The **canary-winged parakeet** (*Brotogeris versicoluorus*) takes his name from the handsome yellow trim on his wings. He is often considered less demanding than the grey-cheek, but also noisier and more nippy.

INDIAN HILL MYNAH

Region of Origin: Southern Asia

Group: Songbird (softbill)—but see below

Size: 9 to 11 inches

Experience Level Needed by Owner: Some experience recommended

Price Range: About $150

PHYSICAL FEATURES

The Indian Hill mynah (*Gracula religiosa*) is easily recognized by his jet-black glossy plumage shaded with iridescent purple. The fleshy yellow wattles on his head are also special features. Males and females look alike.

The mynah is classified in the order Passeriformes—songbirds and perching birds—rather than Psittaciformes—parrots. Thus, the mynah is not really a songbird in the sense that he doesn't sing, but he *is* a perching bird with three toes forward and one back. Actually he is a member of the starling family, which includes those noisy blackish birds who steal seeds from the sparrows at your birdfeeder.

The mynah is as common in India as the starling is in the United States. Mynahs are often kept as pets by Indian natives, and they're considered very useful since they screech whenever snakes slither into the village.

BOLD AND COCKY

Mynahs are extremely proud and courageous, even cocky. They will aggressively defend themselves and their belongings from much larger birds and predators. In the home, they strut boldly around as though they own the place, but then the next minute they clown around and act silly Mynahs are well known for their entertaining, pushy, often rude behaviors.

TALKING ABILITY

The Indian Hill mynah has been called a talking virtuoso, and rightfully so. He is a brilliant imitator, the equal of the talented African grey parrot in his ability to mimic a specific human voice. In marked contrast to other "talking birds" who reproduce human words in their own parrot voices, mynahs and greys reproduce human words in the exact human voice that originally spoke them, including tone, rhythm, and accent.

Actually, the mynah surpasses the grey in his *willingness* to talk—indeed, the biggest problem with mynahs is getting them to shut up! Hundreds of mynahs have been passed from home to home because of their sly insistence on screaming out irrelevant remarks at awkward moments. Mynahs have an uncanny sense for knowing just when your minister or prudish aunt are visiting. They excel at choosing the worst possible things to scream at your audience.

Mynahs also excel at imitating beautiful songs, as well as everyday sounds such as the ringing of the telephone, the creaking of the bathroom door, even the clicking of your typewriter keys. This sounds intriguing at first, but here too the mynah does it to excess. One mynah raised in somebody's wet basement would imitate a sump pump for hours. Even "Frere Jacques" begins to wear thin around the thirty-seventh rendition, especially when you're trying to entertain dinner guests. Mynahs don't seem to know when to quit.

And if you truly want to retain your sanity, never teach a mynah to whistle!

NOISE LEVEL

When mynahs are not mimicking, their chatter is loud, persistent, and annoying. Their normal voice is harsh and penetrating, and they develop a repertoire of shrill whistles, gurgles, squawks, and screeches that can really get on your nerves.

SMALL CAGE = FAT MYNAH

There are many fat mynahs around because of improper caging and lack of exercise. Mynahs are extremely active, but they hop, walk, and fly rather than climb like parrots. They require a cage that measures three feet in all three dimensions. Since it may be hard to find a cage this size, you may have to build it yourself. Fortunately, it doesn't need to be very sturdy, because one saving grace about mynahs is that they don't chew. It's important that the cage material be rustproof, though, since it will require daily washing.

With a diet of commercial mynah pellets, soaked dog food, rice, and fruits and vegetables, you can expect loose droppings. Mynahs are also sloppy eaters, picking up a piece of fruit and whipping their head from side to side. Some of the fruit goes into their mouth, while the rest of it splatters through the cage bars and against your walls. The lower half of the cage should be covered with glass or Plexiglas to keep some of the mess inside the cage.

Also add an eight-inch-square sleeping box and a big clay flowerpot filled with clean water for daily bathing. Be aware, though, that mynahs bathe as enthusiastically as they do everything else; they will flap so happily in the water that everything within reach will be soaked!

WITH OTHER BIRDS

Wild mynahs may live sociably in groups, but pet mynahs will attack other birds; they should not be kept in a community aviary.

HEALTH PROBLEMS

Mynahs are prone to liver disease and bacterial infections, so a liver test and cultures should be done every year.

IS A MYNAH FOR YOU?

Mynah birds require plenty of attention, so they are not a good choice for someone who works all day. You must also ask yourself honestly: will you and everyone else in your family be able to tolerate the raucous noise and extreme messiness?

BUYING A MYNAH

One problem with mynahs is that they do not breed readily in captivity. If you can't find a hand-fed, you'll have to settle for an import. As with all imported birds, mynahs have been captured, sent to USDA import facilities for quarantine, then shipped to pet stores. Thus, the mynah in your pet shop has already endured plenty of handling and stress over several hundred miles of traveling, often under poor conditions.

With imports, a young mynah under six months old should be your only choice. Young mynahs are dull grayish black rather than glossy purplish black, and their pale yellow wattles don't yet flop over onto their neck. After they have molted, their adult colors will appear and you won't be able to tell whether the mynah is one year old or ten.

Older mynahs are more difficult to tame and not as likely to develop into good talkers—unless, of course, they are already tame and talking. If this is the case, you must ask yourself why this "wonderful" mynah is on the market at all.

In General

Mynahs are not as long-lived as other birds of comparable size; although they can live to twenty-five years, most live closer to fifteen or so.

Several Species

There are many species of mynah bird, including common mynahs (*Acridotheres tristis*) who don't talk. The talking mynahs offered as pets, though, are usually Indian Hill mynahs, specifically the **greater Indian Hill** and the **lesser Indian Hill.** The greater is larger, more expensive, and often considered the finest of all talking birds. The lesser is smaller and less expensive, but not as good a talker.

Rainbow lory

LORIES AND LORIKEETS

Region of Origin: Islands of the South Pacific and Australia

Group: Parrot

Size: 10 to 12 inches

Experience Level Needed by Owner: Some experience recommended

Price Range: Most common species cost about $300

PHYSICAL FEATURES

The family of lories and lorikeets are probably the most brilliantly colored parrots of all, with species of deep red, rich blue, stunning violet, and yellow-orange—sometimes all on the same bird. Their glossy, hairlike plumage is similar to that of eclectus parrots, except that both lory sexes are the same splendid combination of colors.

If you have trouble telling lories and lorikeets apart, remember that short tail = short name (lory), while longer tail = longer name (lorikeet). Throughout this profile, we use *lory* to mean either lory or lorikeet.

COLORFUL CLOWNS

To match their bright appearance, lories have equally bright personalities. These intelligent birds are curious about the world and friendly toward everyone. They would never be called introverts. Even wild lories sometimes fly directly toward the tourists in Australia.

Lories are exceptionally bold, lively, and entertaining. They are skilled climbers who love to do somersaults and other comical and acrobatic tricks, so they require roomy cages with lots of perches and interesting toys. Young hand-fed lories thrive on being handled and caressed. They roll around on their backs and wrestle with toys, or perform other clownish antics to solicit attention.

DISCIPLINE THE DEVILS!

Lories don't usually become screamers, but because they can be willful birds, you must be firm and consistent with discipline. Most lories have a devilish glint somewhere in their bright eyes, and some individuals become nippy at maturity. Like caiques and conures, they are high-energy birds who like to keep busy, so they may develop the habit of nipping while you're holding them. Offer your lory a toy to nibble on while he's on your hand—this gives him a substitute for your fingers!

Note: If you do teach your lory to perch on your hand or wrist, be prepared: these birds grip very tightly with needle-sharp nails.

SPECIAL FEEDING AND BATHING NEEDS

Lories have one very unusual physical feature: they are called brush-tongued parrots because their tongue ends in a bundle of hairlike structures that form a little brush. This brush is used for licking their natural foods: nectar, pollen, and soft fruits.

Unfortunately, since "you are what you eat," this soft, high-sugar diet has predictable results: foul-smelling fluid droppings that make an enormous mess. For many years this major drawback meant that lories had to be housed outdoors, since they have the unpleasant habit of squirting their droppings powerfully through their cage bars, all over your floor and walls.

Today, a powdered commercial mixture (Lories Delight) has been developed to thicken the droppings. Mixed with fruits and vegetables, this excellent diet solves much of the cleaning problem, but many lories are still housed in solid-sided acrylic cages, or in barred cages flared out at the bottom. You can also purchase a flared apron to fit around the bottom portion of your lory's cage. Fortunately, these messy birds love to bathe, so offer them a permanent bathing dish filled with clean water.

CHATTERERS

Most lories converse with a loud chatter that can be annoying. Most are not great talkers, but the larger species may mimic a few words or sounds.

BUYING A LORY

Buy a young hand-fed from six weeks to nine months old. When choosing, keep in mind that all lories should be very active (sometimes hyperactive), not sedentary. It would not be normal to see a lory standing quietly.

WITH OTHER BIRDS

To provide companionship and to double the fun of lory-owning, lories are often kept in pairs, but only two to a cage. Lories are not candidates for a community aviary. They are fearless and aggressive with other parrots, and the larger lories can and will kill other species or even new birds of their own species.

IN GENERAL

Most lories live fifteen to thirty years.

SPECIES

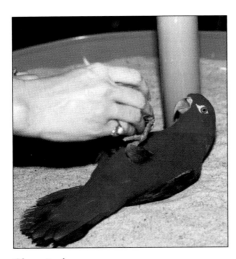

Chattering lory

There are over thirty species of lories in captivity. Most have typical lory personalities—lively and cheerful—so you can essentially choose the color and type of voice you prefer. Since everyone's taste is different, you'll need to see the birds and hear the different voices before choosing. Don't feel restricted by this sample group. If you like what you've heard about lories, feel free to give every species an equal look.

The most popular species include the **chattering** (*Lorius garulus*), a noisy lory, but an excellent talker; and the **red** or **moluccan** (*Eos bornea*), one of the larger lories, quite playful, although noisy. These two hardy species may even consent to eat a normal pellet diet with some nectar and greens. Quieter lories include the **rainbow** (*Trichoglossus haematodus*), a lorikeet mosaic of magnificent colors; the **blue-streaked** (*Eos reticulata*); and **Goldie's** (*Psitteuteles goldiei*), a small, gentle lorikeet with a low voice.

Peach-faced lovebirds

LOVEBIRDS

Region of Origin: Africa

Group: Parrot

Size: 6 inches

Experience Level Needed by Owner: Fine for the novice

Price Range: $20 to $40

PHYSICAL FEATURES

The coloration of lovebirds is striking—some combination of light to olive green, peachy salmon pink, bright blue, pastel yellow, and/or stark black. They're about the same size as a budgie, but with a stouter body and a short rounded tail.

ACROBATIC CLOWNS

Lovebirds are cheerful, engaging, amusing clowns. Because they are agile and acrobatic, with boundless energy, they need a cage that is at least eighteen inches in all three dimensions and plenty of hanging toys and swings. These little dynamos seldom stop moving.

Lovebirds are also chewers who delight in shredding paper and cardboard, which includes books and photographs and letters to your mother. Keep an eye on these curious birds when you let them loose, and provide them with milk cartons to sleep in and eventually tear to shreds.

ROWDY RASCALS

For all their playfulness, lovebirds are seldom called "sweet and gentle"; "rowdy and rascally" are more commonly used to describe them! These are confident, assertive little birds who tend to bite as they go through their juvenile period. Even after this period, some lovebirds remain a bit nippy.

Indeed, if you want a cuddly bird, a lovebird may not be your best choice. These birds have independent spirits and strong minds of their own. They enjoy flying to your shoulder and climbing up your arm, but they may take off if you try to pet them. Lovebirds require more effort to tame than some other parrotlike birds in their size range. Still, if you're attracted to a feisty, fearless, energetic personality in a tiny body, you can't beat a lovebird!

HAND-FED VERSUS PARENT-RAISED

If you are interested in taming, you must search diligently for a young, hand-fed lovebird. Hand-feds are so different from parent-raised lovebirds that they are almost a different species!

Parent-raised lovebirds resist taming. They demand everything their own way and bite hard. If you're interested in aviary birds, parent-raised lovebirds are fine. But if you want an affectionate pet, you must find a hand-fed and handle him every single day, because lovebirds quickly revert to the wild without daily interaction. If all this is done, you'll have a dynamic and adorable little pet.

Unfortunately, hand-fed lovebirds are hard to find. The low prices that they bring to breeders means that hand-feeding is simply not worth the extra time and effort to them. Some breeders do specialize in producing good pets, though, so look for them. Lovebirds under six months old have softer colors and a partly black beak.

NOISY BIRDS

Compared to other parrots, lovebirds are more annoying than loud. Their chirps are sharp and insistent, and their call is rather piercing. Very few lovebirds will talk.

WITH OTHER BIRDS

It is a myth that lovebirds must be kept in pairs or they will die. Lovebirds are not called lovebirds for their sweetness, but simply for their habit of huddling together in a row. But when they're not huddling, they're usually bullying each other. Lovebirds are not very tolerant of other birds. Sometimes a pair does become devoted to each other, but more often they are spiteful and quarrelsome.

Lovebirds are not suitable for community aviaries, either. They may attack weak or sickly birds, or even new additions to their cage. These reckless little devils will even challenge larger birds. Thus, single lovebirds make the best pets. Paired lovebirds seldom tame well.

MALE OR FEMALE?

Females generally have less desirable temperaments. They are quite "nesty," tearing up and shredding their newspaper and laying empty eggs. Unfortunately, the sex of a lovebird can't be told by appearance or color. However, if you see a lovebird tucking nesting material (such as newspaper) into its back feathers, you know you're looking at a female.

IN GENERAL

Lovebirds usually live ten to twenty years.

Peach-faced lovebird (*Agapornis roseicollis*)

This is the most common variety and makes the best all-around pet. The normal color is green with a peachy, salmon, or reddish face, but the peach-faced lovebird comes in over thirty color mutations—more than any other parrot. These include pied (patched), blue, cinnamon, lutino (yellow), white, and silver.

Some fanciers feel that color is tied to temperament. They report that the normal greens are bold, curious, comical, vocal—and the worst biters. Blues and blue pieds, they say, are gentler and make excellent pets.

Masked lovebird (*Agapornis personatus*)

These are also called eye-ring lovebirds since they wear a thick white ring around each eye. The most common mask colors are black and blue. Most breeders recommend that you keep peach-faced lovebirds separate from eye-ring lovebirds, as they often fight when mixed together.

Macaws

Region of Origin: Central and South America, and Mexico

Group: Parrot

Size: 26 to 40 inches for large macaws; 11 to 19 inches for dwarf macaws

Experience Level Needed by Owner: For large macaws, plenty of experience is strongly recommended; for dwarf macaws, some experience is recommended

Price Range: $800 to $1200 (except for the magnificent hyacinth macaw, which costs about $10,000)

Scarlet macaw

PHYSICAL FEATURES

These are your classic jungle birds or tropical birds, seen in every Caribbean travel brochure: vividly hued parrots with formidable beaks and long pointed tails. A special feature of macaws is the naked whitish-pinkish skin covering their cheeks. Some species also have delicate war-paint stripes across their cheeks. Macaws have a bold, commanding eye that is immediately impressive, but also intimidating to novices.

THE LARGEST PARROTS OF ALL

In tropical America, macaws live in large groups along riverbanks, often very high in the trees and many hundreds of feet above sea level. They are the largest, most powerful parrots in the world.

ARE THEY BITERS?

Probably the first macaw question asked by novices is, "Do they bite?" Yes, macaws do bite. Like most large parrots, they bite when they're frightened, angry, or jealous. If you are not their favorite person, or if you are a stranger and you try to force yourself on them, they may bite. If you threaten or tease them in any way or invade their personal territory, they may bite. Macaws who have been mistreated in the past are especially quick to retaliate.

Though a macaw's beak may be tremendously powerful, it is also extremely sensitive. Most macaws retain precise control over everything they do with their beak. In other words, if you provoke a macaw, he will do what he feels is justified for the situation. He may deliver a crushing blow, an aching squeeze, a painful pinch, or a dainty nip. Every macaw "bite" is not going to send you to the hospital emergency room with a severed finger!

In spite of their striking facial markings and bold posturing, most macaws are not serious biters. When raised with kindness and disciplined with nurturing dominance, macaws are quite gentle. Trainers love working with macaws because they are honest birds. They usually give you plenty of warning when they are upset. They shriek, raise their wings or crown feathers, or open their beak and slash it at the air.

It's also important to understand that macaws enjoy exploring with their beaks, especially young macaws. If a macaw closes his beak around your wrist, he may be trying to keep his balance by using his beak as a third hand, or he may simply be fascinated by your glittering watch. Gentle young macaws have been turned into defensive biters by people who slapped at their big beaks whenever they tried to explore.

Still, let no one doubt that their enormous power must be respected. Never reach out to touch a strange macaw, and never allow your children to do this. Respectful children and macaws mix fine, but rowdy children and macaws do not. A macaw could seriously mutilate your child's hand—or your own hand—if provoked or feeling grumpy.

THE PLAYFUL MACAW

Macaws are not generally described as cuddly, but rather as playful and clever. They climb all over their cages, hang upside down, and do somersaults. These clever birds are willing and able to learn complicated tricks, such as riding bikes and running a flag up a flagpole.

Macaws require large cages—the bigger the better, but at least four feet wide by two feet deep by five feet high. They must be able to flap their wings. Because so much of their play is carried out with their beaks and because of their tremendous chewing strength, their toys must be ultra heavy-duty and hung from strong chains. The bars of the cage must be extremely strong because these birds will literally bend them until they snap.

When they're not playing, macaws are some of the best large parrots to perch on T-stands. Since they are primarily climbing rather than flying birds, they are usually content to remain on the stand. However, never leave them unsupervised because the third "personality" word for macaws is destructive. Your house will never look the same again.

FOR EXPERIENCED OWNERS ONLY

The large macaws are not suitable choices for a first bird, and they are not suitable for the average home. They are too intelligent and need too much room and proper training. If you raise them sensibly by setting rules and teaching verbal commands, you'll be fine. But if you're afraid of them or if you don't read and respond correctly to their body language, a macaw will dominate you. He may become an aggressive screamer who is difficult to handle.

Macaws demand lots of attention and use bizarre methods to obtain it. They slide back and forth along their perch, sway from side to side, swing their head in an odd figure eight pattern, and utter peculiar noises.

Macaws who are neglected, bored, mistreated, or otherwise not handled properly often become feather pluckers. There is no sorrier sight than a huge, powerful macaw reduced to a bony skeleton while his splendidly colored feathers lay strewn all over the surrounding floor.

HARSH VOICES

Macaws will often learn to say a few words and phrases, but they are not usually skilled mimics. Their voice is loud and harsh, and they seldom give up their natural parrot sounds. If you have close neighbors, you should not have a large macaw. These big birds don't hesitate to express themselves with harsh squawking and shrieking, and like all large parrots, they usually engage in daily screaming periods.

STAY AWAY FROM IMPORTS

As with all large parrots, the best pets are domestic hand-feds about four months old and fully weaned. Deforestation in Central and South America has caused populations of wild macaws to diminish at an alarming rate—several macaw species are officially endangered or threatened—but macaws can still be legally imported. There are many imports on the market; these should not be chosen as pets.

HYBRIDS

Some breeders deliberately produce hybrid macaws with unusual coloring. This creates a mish-mash of traits and characteristics, some of which may be wildly conflicting. Since no one knows which traits have been passed on from which species, these breedings are always hit-and-miss—sometimes the negative traits from both species come over. The continued survival of macaw species is shaky enough without mixing species and diluting their valuable genes. I recommend that you stay far away from hybrid macaws—and from the breeders who deliberately produce them.

MALE OR FEMALE?

Some breeders feel that the sexes are virtually identical in behavior, while other breeders feel that males are a bit calmer and females a bit feistier.

HEALTH PROBLEMS

Macaws are susceptible to a debilitating illness called macaw wasting disease. The common parrot disease psittacosis is also a potential problem.

IN GENERAL

Macaws usually live sixty to eighty years.

Blue-and-gold macaw (*Ara ararauna*)

This popular species is probably the most intelligent and affectionate of all macaws. He is exceedingly handsome: his upper parts are a rich turquoise blue with a greenish haze, his lower parts are yellowish gold.

The blue-and-gold is a talented mimic who can develop a respectable vocabulary (for a macaw), but is mostly prized for his whimsical personality and clownish acrobatics. This lovable extrovert is always eager to rise to social occasions—no audience is too small or too large for his antics. And if any macaw could be called cuddly, it would be the blue-and-gold.

But be forewarned that he has a sly sense of humor and enjoys making his owner the butt of little tricks. If you can handle the special needs of all macaws, hand-fed blue-and-golds make delightful pets.

Scarlet macaw (*Ara macao*)

The scarlet macaw is one of the most instantly recognizable of all parrots: vivid red, with some combination of yellow, green, and/or blue on his wings and tail. His total length can reach three feet, but half of that is his incredibly long tail. Scarlets often end up with frayed tails because other birds sneak up and nibble on it!

The temperament of the scarlet macaw is a topic of controversy. Some fanciers believe that the scarlet can be hyperactive and does not make a very good pet, that he often becomes aggressive when mature, and that of all the macaws, he has the greatest potential for behavior problems, including screaming and feather plucking.

Other fanciers defend him just as strongly. They believe that scarlets are simply more impressionable and more sensitive to early neglect or mistreatment. This species is not as quick—nor as able—to forgive and forget. If raised in isolation or slapped when young, he is harder to rehabilitate than other parrots. These fanciers say that scarlets may be headstrong, but they were usually made that way by improper handling.

Fanciers disagree about his talking ability as well. Some feel that the scarlet is equal to the blue-and-gold, while others label him "fair at best."

Green-winged macaw (*Ara chloropterus*)

The green-wing has to be one of the worst-named of all parrots. Yes, he has some green on his wings, but his main color is crimson red. In fact, at first glance he looks almost identical to the scarlet macaw! Distinguish the green-wing by his larger size, shorter tail, war-paint stripes on his cheeks, and no yellow coloring.

The green-wing's temperament is less in dispute than the scarlet's. Most breeders use words like *docile*, *placid*, *mellow*, and *affectionate* to describe this macaw. Green-wings adore people, they enjoy social interaction and handling, and they love to learn tricks and show off. They are excellent pets for active families who can handle the special needs of all macaws. Some fanciers believe that the green-wing is the smartest of all macaws.

Along with pure-bred green-wings, though, you'll find lots of green-wing hybrids for sale. Stay away from these—you have no idea what combination of traits you're getting.

Military macaw (*Ara militaris*)

This macaw probably takes his name from his dull green plumage. Because of his muted colors, he has always been underrated as a pet, and this is a shame. Although he is not a good talker, he is easygoing and adaptable to family life. Some are rather independent, while others are so sociable they are constantly underfoot "helping." Note that a lot of militaries have been smuggled into this country.

Red-fronted macaw (*Ara rubrogenys*)

The red-front is relatively new to captivity, but is reported to be exuberant and affectionate with his own family. He's smaller than other macaws and quicker on his feet. It will be interesting to see how his popularity grows in the United States.

Hyacinth macaw (*Anodorhynchus hyacinthinus*)

Once you have been privileged to see this splendid giant, you will never forget him. First-time viewers always gape at the luxuriant cobalt blue color, the brilliant yellow eye ring, the huge black overhanging beak, and the bright yellow stripe that curves along his beak like a whimsical smile. It's hard to believe that something that looks like an enormous stuffed toy could be real!

Hyacinths, the largest parrots in existence, live in eastern Brazilian and Bolivian jungle. Approaching four feet in length and exceeding a four-foot wingspan, hyacinths are extremely powerful. But despite their forbidding appearance, they are the most docile macaws of all. Hand-fed hyacinths are so sweet and trusting that they are easily tamed. They enjoy handling and cuddling and display few behavior problems. They are not usually gifted talkers, but they *will* freely use their loud, piercing voice to chatter and shriek.

So if your heart yearns for the biggest macaw of all, if you have plenty of space and free time, and if you have nine or ten thousand dollars to spend, a hyacinth may appeal to you. Note, however, that because these magnificent birds are so scarce in the wild, those who are taken should be used in captive breeding programs. With the hyacinth's very existence on the line, it may be irresponsible and selfish to keep one simply as a pet.

DWARF OR MINI MACAW

Severe macaw

Still interested in an intelligent, playful macaw, but don't have enough space for a thirty-inch bird? Or perhaps you're intimidated by the powerful beaks of one of the "big boys." If so, the eleven- to nineteen-inch dwarf macaws are a good compromise.

But if you're hoping for a brilliant scarlet macaw in miniature, you won't find one among the dwarfs. Dwarf macaws are not brightly colored; they're mostly green with a few colored markings. They do, however, have the same bare facial area that sets the large macaws apart from other parrots.

Dwarf macaws are more manageable than large macaws, but they would still not be described as shy. These hardy birds are extroverts who thrive

Noble macaw

on attention. They may mimic a few words, although not very clearly. The voice of these macaws is not as powerful as that of their larger cousins, but unfortunately they make up for it by being twice as exuberant and twice as noisy!

The **severe macaw** (*Ara severa*) is the largest dwarf. With war-paint stripes on his cheeks, he is the one who most closely resembles a large macaw.

The **yellow-collared macaw** (*Ara auricollis*) is the one most frequently bred in captivity and makes a delightful pet.

The **noble** or **Hahn's macaw** (*Ara nobilis*) is a very small, outgoing macaw, smaller than some conures. The Hahn's can even perch on your finger!

PARROTLETS

Region of Origin: Central and South America

Group: Parrot

Size: 5 inches

Experience Level Needed by Owner: Some experience recommended

Price Range: $100; you must buy a pair

Pacific parrotlet

PHYSICAL FEATURES

These tiny birds are the smallest of all parrots commonly sold as pets. Most parrotlet species are green or yellow-green, with stocky builds and short wedge-shaped tails. In most species, males also have some blue feathers.

ACTIVE AND SHY

Although parrotlets don't breed readily in captivity, you should search hard for a domestic baby, preferably hand-fed. Domestics are hardy birds who are easy to tame, while imports are often nervous and have a nasty bite. All parrotlets are extremely active and somewhat shy. They are unlikely to sit on your finger for very long, so they're more interesting and amusing to observe than to play with. Parrotlets should always be kept in pairs, as they are very devoted to each other.

QUIET VOICE

Parrotlets have a quiet voice. Some hand-feds may mimic a few words, but they are more skilled at imitating sounds such as sneezing, coughing, and whistling.

The most popular parrotlet, and the one most commonly bred in captivity, is the **pacific** or **celestial** (*Forpus coelestis*). Other parrotlet species with a similar appearance and temperament are the **turquoise-rumped** (*Forpus cyanopygius*) and the **green-rumped** (*Forpus passerinus*).

PEKIN ROBIN

Region of Origin: China, India, and Burma

Group: Songbird (softbill)

Size: 6 inches

Experience Level Needed by Owner: Fine for the novice

Price Range: $40 each; you must buy a pair

PHYSICAL FEATURES

These colorful little birds (*Leiothrix lutea*) are grayish-brown with a golden yellow breast and some red on their wings.

THE BEST SOFTBILL FOR THE NOVICE

Within the songbird group, there are many softbill members, but Pekin robins are the best choice for the beginning softbill owner. They are strong, active, and amusing, and not difficult to keep. Although they must be fed a commercial insectile mixture and fruit slices, they may also eat seed and are not as fussy about food as some other softbills. Pekin robins are lively, hardy little birds who become quite tame and trusting. They are a good choice for someone who wants a colorful songbird, but something a little different from a canary or finch.

A BIT MESSY

Since their soft food moves through their intestinal system quickly, Pekin robins have soft droppings, so the cage should be cleaned daily.

One Pair per Roomy Cage

Since these birds are active and love to flit about, they require a roomy cage: two to three feet long, two feet high, and one and a half feet deep. They adore their mate and should always be purchased as a pair, but one pair only because two pairs will fight. Pekins sometimes quarrel with other species as well. In large community aviaries, they are sometimes mixed with canaries and finches of similar size, but they should not be kept with smaller finches.

Melodious Song

The male Pekin robin has such a sweet, melodious song that the best method of sexing is to listen for his voice. These little birds also twitter and call pleasantly to each other, but when excited they are capable of uttering loud rattling calls.

PIONUS PARROTS

Region of Origin: South America

Group: Parrot

Size: 10 to 12 inches

Experience Level Needed by Owner: Fine for the novice

Price Range: $100 to $500

Blue-headed pionus

PHYSICAL FEATURES

Pionus parrots resemble small chubby Amazons, but you can distinguish them by their short square tails with red coloring underneath. And pionus may resemble Amazons in appearance, but it's a big mistake to consider these parrots as small substitutes. In personality, pionus are very different from their South American cousins.

EXTREMELY GENTLE PARROTS

Because pionus are so steady and trustworthy, they are often recommended as children's pets. They seldom bite (although they will chew enthusiastically on their perches and toys), and their personality is calm, sweet, and mellow, but still fun. They are responsive to handling, and they will usually go to anyone who approaches them slowly and calmly. However, they are easily stressed or frightened, and may then make an odd wheezing sound that sounds like an asthma attack. All they need is peace and quiet to calm down.

Pionus do share one trait with Amazons: they tend to put on weight when they don't get enough exercise. Provide your pionus with a roomy cage and a well-stocked playground. Keep an eye on them, though, because pionus do like to climb down and run around the floor, where they could be stepped on.

Even Older Pionus Are Tameable

Pionus do not breed well in captivity, so imported pionus are very common. Although many of these are gentler than other species of imported parrots, they seldom enjoy being touched or handled, so look carefully for a domestic hand-fed. A young hand-fed pionus is extremely easy to tame. An older pionus who was hand-fed as a baby may also settle down nicely.

Quiet Voices

Pionus parrots have chattery voices, but are considered relatively screech-free. Most are not good talkers, but some will mimic a few words, usually in a low voice.

In General

As mid-size parrots, pionus make more practical pets than the larger parrots. They have full parrot personalities, yet they're not too big for an apartment. They don't have intimidating beaks or heavy claws. They don't have dominant personalities or screaming voices that demand you pay attention to them; pionus are happy to play with their toys while you're gone.

I hope more prospective owners will consider these appealing birds, because pionus are well-suited to the average family and the average home. They are an excellent choice for people who love the typical parrot "look," but would rather do without the demanding requirements and potential behavioral problems.

Several Species to Choose From

The most popular pionus is the **white-capped** (*Pionus senilis*), followed by the **blue-headed** (*Pionus menstruus*) and the **maximilian** (*Pionus maximiliani*). Other fine choices, if you can find them, include the **dusky** (*Pionus fuscus*) and the **bronze-winged** (*Pionus chalcopterus*). All pionus species have similar temperaments.

Quaker Parrot

Region of Origin: South America

Group: Parrot

Size: 12 inches

Experience Level Needed by Owner: Some experience recommended

Price Range: $100 to $150

Physical Features

This greenish parrot (*Myiopsitta monachus*), also called monk parakeet, is named for his unusual gray bib, reminiscent of the old-fashioned Quaker costume pictured on the Quaker Oats box.

Wild Colonies

Quakers have established themselves as wild birds in some states, but since they live in colonies and damage crops and fruit trees, they are not always welcomed. In fact, some agricultural states have banned them as pets because of the risk of their escaping. Instead of roosting in single nests or hollowed-out trees, Quakers cooperate to weave together a unique community stick nest that rests on heavy branches and weighs up to several hundred pounds!

Lovable and Playful

Quakers have been described as lovable birds in a small noisy package. They are affectionate, peaceful, and amusing, and enjoy doing tricks. Since their active behavior is often compared to that of conures, they require a roomy cage: about two feet in all three dimensions. Offer plenty of wooden chew toys, cardboard boxes, and empty paper towel rolls to shred. Some Quakers will try to weave shredded newspapers into the bars of their cage!

Quakers enjoy some free playtime, but must always be supervised. They love to chew and will not differentiate between your belongings and their own toys. They are entranced by shiny objects and are forever filching and hiding jewelry, coins, and bits of aluminum foil, all of which are dangerous to them.

GOOD TALKERS . . . EXCELLENT SCREECHERS

Quakers love attention so much that they will shriek to get it. They can be noisy birds with a loud voice. On the plus side, if you purchase a single, domestic hand-fed who has just been weaned, he will probably learn to say a few words and even imitate the sounds of wild outdoor birds. These intelligent birds are quick to pick up new phrases and many have extremely clear voices for a bird of their size.

IN GENERAL

Although some Quakers make it into their late teens, most live about twelve years. Combine their cheerful personality with a convenient size, and you have an interesting parrot to consider as a pet.

SENEGAL PARROT

Region of Origin: Africa

Group: Parrot

Size: 9 inches

Experience Level Needed by Owner: Some experience recommended

Price Range: $200 to $300

PHYSICAL FEATURES

Senegals (*Poicephalus senegalus*) are lovely short-tailed parrots, mostly green with a dark gray head and bright yellow-orange belly. Subspecies have different degrees of yellow or orange shading on their underside.

ENERGETIC AND BOLD

Senegals are generally quite energetic. They clamber all over their cage, hang upside down, and fling their toys around. Senegals who are confined too much become lethargic, so they need plenty of time on a well-stocked playground. Supervision is essential while they are out because they will be delighted to forage through your possessions and chew them up with their strong, busy beaks.

Because Senegals have strong personalities, they can be nippy when something goes against their liking. But when hand-raised and purchased young, most Senegals make affectionate, appealing, and clever pets. They are especially good for people who are looking to move up from a smaller bird.

It is important to accustom young Senegals to changes in routine because, like African greys, Senegals sometimes have strong reactions to stress. They should be moved around the house so they're comfortable in all areas, and handled by several different people. Otherwise, they may become one-person birds.

Senegals can be very bold birds who act very fierce when protecting what is "theirs." They may take great delight in running after a big dog and chasing it into another room or jumping onto the backs of larger parrots.

Young Hand-Feds Only!

Pet Senegals should always be hand-raised. Young domestic hand-feds are easily tamed, while older and imported birds make disappointing pets, remaining wild and nervous. However, even a hand-fed Senegal should be handled daily if he is to retain his tameness. But don't worry; if you should forget to handle him, your sociable Senegal will probably remind you by calling you and flapping his wings for attention!

Distinguish young Senegals by their eyes: the dark color changes to yellow between six months and one year of age. Both sexes look alike, but there seem to be more males born than females.

Perhaps Two Dozen Words

Senegals try hard to learn to speak, and some may mimic up to two dozen words, but their voice sounds squeaky and computerlike. Some are better at imitating sounds or whistling. Since loudness is relative, Senegals are much quieter than Amazons, macaws, and cockatoos.

In General

Similar African parrots, although not that commonly seen, include **Meyer's parrot** (*Poicephalus meyeri*) and the **red-bellied parrot** (*Poicephalus rufiventris*). Even less common are **Jardine's parrot** (*Poicephalus gulielmi*) and the **brown-headed parrot** (*Poicephalus cryptoxanthus*). All these birds make good pets.

As mid-size parrots, the Senegal and his cousins make more practical pets than the larger and more demanding parrots. They're sized right and have full parrot personalities, and are well suited to the average family and the average home.

Step Three

FINDING YOUR BIRD

4

SOURCES OF BIRDS

Once you've chosen a species—or perhaps narrowed your choices to two or three—where should you begin looking for your bird?

You have two general choices: you can buy your bird from a local source, or you can have one shipped from a distant source. Shipping means that a distant breeder or bird store will select a bird for you, secure the bird in a shipping crate, put the crate on a plane, and you'll meet the crate at your end of the flight. Is this a good idea?

Not really, especially for the novice bird owner. You should take an up-close, personal look at any bird before committing yourself. You must be able to evaluate the bird's personality and to predict how well you and he will get along. Shipping is the way that most pet shops receive their birds, and it's stressful to the bird. Many breeders refuse to ship, out of concern that something might go wrong. This concern is justifiable, as tragedies can and do occur when shipping animals. So before resorting to shipping, you should exhaust every possible source in your own city, county, state—and neighboring states!

How Do You Find Local Sources?

1. Check your Yellow Pages for bird specialty stores, usually listed under *Birds* or *Aviaries*. Some businesses under *Pet Stores* might specify birds as their specialty. Bird specialty stores should not be confused with general pet shops. Bird specialty stores sell only birds and bird supplies. Some even breed their own birds and offer wonderful hand-raised babies. Ask the bird store if they have your chosen species and also if they know of any upcoming events such as bird fairs, expos, or shows. Make sure to check the phone books of neighboring communities as well, because you may have to travel to find a good bird specialty store.

2. Call your local newsstands, bird stores, and pet supply shops to see if they carry *Bird Talk* (monthly) or *Birds USA* (annual). These magazines have many classified ads for breeders and bird stores, and often some event listings. Another magazine is *American Cage Bird*, which may be harder to find; it's geared more to experienced breeders and exhibitors than to novice or prospective owners, but it does carry a lot of advertising.

Read all ads carefully, and avoid those where the wording indicates that the dealer is a wholesale bird mill churning out lots of different species for distribution to pet shops. The best breeder for you is informally known as a hobby breeder rather than a quantity breeder. The hobby breeder specializes in only a few species and offers hand-fed babies directly from his home to yours.

Also look for such animal-related tabloids as *The Pet & Horse Exchange*, *Animal Review*, or *The Pet Owner's Weekly Journal*. You'll often find these offered for free at pet shops and pet supply stores. They sometimes carry ads for birds and upcoming bird events.

3. Check under *Veterinarians* in your Yellow Pages to see if any vets list birds as their specialty. You won't find many. Experienced bird owners often travel some distance to have their birds seen by an avian vet whom they've come to trust. Since avian vets are few and far between, look through the Yellow Pages of neighboring communities as well as your own. Call the avian vets and ask if they know of any breeders of your chosen species. Some avian vets are breeders themselves.

If you're striking out with the avian vets, call the general vets, as well. You may get lucky and find an all-animal vet who just happens to know a breeder of the species you're looking for. Also ask every vet if he or she knows of any upcoming bird fairs, expos, or shows.

4. Fairs, expos, and shows. These are wondrous events for a prospective bird owner to attend. Here is a large gathering of hobby breeders with pet birds for sale. Their birds have often been hand-fed and hand-raised, their prices are usually excellent, and they have a good selection of baby birds for you to choose from, either at the show or back at their home or aviary.

Most breeders won't pressure you into buying a bird, but just in case, don't get carried away by a breeder's glowing descriptions of his birds. Don't let any breeder talk you into a species that you know from your research is not right for you. Be affable, but a hard sell.

Bird events are often held at local fairgrounds, so you might try calling the fairgrounds to see if they have anything "birdie" booked for the future.

5. Earlier, when I recommended buying your bird locally, your first thought was probably your local pet shop. But as you walk in the door, keep in mind that though the owners may be nice and helpful, they may not know much about birds. Because they have spread themselves so thin with so many different types of pets, and because their employees are often well-meaning but inexperienced students or part-timers, they may unintentionally pass along misinformation and rumor rather than facts.

It's unlikely that the store's owners have bred the birds themselves. It's more likely that they've had the birds shipped in. Ask. If they haven't bred the birds, you won't be able to assess the actual breeder's knowledge or experience. You won't have any background on the birds, and you may not have much help in determining true age or sex.

Still, if your chosen species is a budgie, finch, canary, cockatiel, or lovebird, you can certainly check out local pet shops. Be sure to carefully examine all the birds in the shop for signs of illness, not just the particular bird you're considering. Communicable diseases may not show up until after you've gotten your bird home. Ask to see breeder records that confirm the bird's age.

You might be wondering about the kind of "pet shop" found in discount department stores. This is where Grandma purchased her canaries: you remember, the old, malnourished, stressed-out canaries who died in a year or two. Never buy a bird from a department store.

All of this careful searching may seem like a lot of work, but one of the most important characteristics you are seeking in your bird is quality. What is quality? A bird may be of good quality, poor quality, or something in between.

A bird of good quality is healthy and vibrant. He doesn't attack people who walk past his cage, nor does he hide in the corner of his cage. He is a good representative of his species, with most of its typical characteristics.

A reputable breeder is one who produces quality birds by choosing his breeding pairs carefully and raising his babies with extra-loving care, often by hand in his own living room. A good breeder searches for the best home for each baby, asking probing questions about the prospective buyer's ability to properly care for the baby.

You'll soon be a buyer yourself, so don't be put off by such questions. You're not buying a piece of merchandise, but a small living creature who has been carefully bred and lovingly raised by a concerned, dedicated breeder. This is exactly the type of good breeder from whom you want to buy your bird.

How about buying from private parties, such as friends, neighbors, or co-workers? Suppose a friend or colleague says, "I'm going to be moving soon and I can't take my cockatoo to my new apartment. He's a great bird—want to see him?"

There's always the danger that your personal or work relationship could suffer if you buy a bird from someone you know well and the bird doesn't work out. But the biggest danger is that your colleague may have a "problem bird" that he's desperate to unload. This is especially true if claims made about the bird sound too good to be true. "He's a great talker . . . does tricks . . . loves to cuddle . . . healthy as a horse . . . quiet as a mouse . . ." Great birds are not that easy to come by. Why are these people willing to get rid of such a "great" bird?

Triple cautions apply to classified ads by people you don't know. "Senegal parrot for sale, talks and whistles." "Moluccan cockatoo, gorgeous, tame, loves people." "Green-wing macaw, wonderful pet, large cage included." When you call these people, you'll hear a dozen different reasons why these "wonderful" birds are on the market: "We're moving to Georgia and he won't like the heat." "We have a new baby who takes up too much of our time." "He doesn't like my mother-in-law."

You're unlikely to hear these reasons: "He chews." "He shrieks." "He bites." "He plucks his feathers." "He attacks other birds."

Secondhand birds can be very risky buys, especially from unknown sources. Private parties are often so desperate to unload their bird that they'll say anything to convince you to buy. But they may be as inexperienced as you are, and may not really know much about their own bird. In fact, their improper handling may have caused the bird's problems. They may not know that, so they'll make up other reasons why the bird is acting the way he is.

On the practical side, an important consideration for many prospective buyers is money. Private-party birds are often offered at low prices that are hard to pass up. But what kind of bird will you be getting? Maybe the worst quality bird in the world; maybe the best quality bird in the world. The biggest disadvantage of secondhand birds is unpredictability.

If your budget is very tight, you can certainly go look, but you must go in with your eyes open, not just your heart. The bird is probably an adult and quite possibly an import—in just a moment, we'll discuss the implications of both of these factors. In any case, you're taking a gamble in the most important areas of health and behavior. Since private party sales are always *caveat emptor,* with no warranties required, you must insist upon a written health guarantee. Chapters 5 and 6 discuss guarantees further, as well as the specific questions you should ask the owner and the examinations you should give the bird. Be extra-careful that a secondhand bird passes with flying colors.

The satisfaction that comes from giving a neglected or unhappy bird a loving home may be worth the extra effort and risk. Good birds are everywhere, if only you know how to recognize them—and then how to handle them properly.

As you're collecting your list of sources, you'll read through classified ads and start coming across terms you don't understand. Let's interpret some of that jargon.

DOMESTIC OR IMPORT

"Eclectus parrots, domestic-bred!" The phrase *domestic-bred* is so important that if it's not mentioned in the ad, the first question you should ask on the phone is: "Is he a domestic bird or an import?"

Unlike our dogs and cats, who are almost always born in the United States, pet birds may be born in the United States (domestic-bred) or born wild in another country and imported into the United States.

A domestic bird should always be your choice for a pet. A domestic bird was born in captivity and is accustomed to confinement; he knows no other way of life. He is friendly and trusting with people. He is familiar with our country, our climate, our foods, and our language. He is usually healthy, since he hasn't been exposed to foreign parasites or bacteria. He is by far your best chance for a good, happy pet.

In contrast, an imported bird was born in the jungles or forests or open grasslands of South and Central America, the Caribbean, South Pacific Islands, Asia, or Africa. He had to fly or scramble frantically away as determined natives chased after him with nets. Once captured, he was kept in a filthy shack on a dirt floor crawling with parasites. On his long trip to the United States, he was crowded together with other terrified birds and offered only strange seeds to eat. At the USDA quarantine center, he was housed in an isolation cage for another thirty days.

So that pet-shop import who has "just" arrived from abroad has already been severely stressed by malnutrition and physical and mental trauma. His entire way of life has been stolen. He will be susceptible to digestive upsets and viral, bacterial, and parasitic infections for a long time. You will probably never know his true age. You won't know his background or habits, but you will know that he has struggled against humans, shrieked at them, perhaps slashed at them with his beak and claws—all in trying to defend himself and his freedom.

Training an import to overcome a natural fear or aggression takes an enormous amount of time, effort, and patience; even then, many never gain full confidence in humans. Your import may learn to talk, he may learn complicated tricks, he may learn to cuddle, but his mind and his heart will always be wild.

And remember that all these problems develop through the *legal* importation of birds. Some birds are smuggled into this country to avoid importation costs and/or because they are so endangered that importation is no longer legal. Smuggled birds are even more traumatized than legal imports because they have been handled by the greediest and most uncaring hands possible.

More important, since the birds bypassed the USDA quarantine stations, they pose a health menace to every other bird in this country. The USDA requires a thirty-day quarantine for good reason: to test for communicable diseases. Newcastle disease is a dreaded viral infection so contagious that it could literally wipe out America's pet birds and the entire poultry industry. The infectious parrot disease psittacosis poses a threat to pet birds *and* humans.

The way to avoid these health, behavioral, and moral problems is to buy only birds born and raised in the United States.

CLOSE-BANDED

What if the person selling the bird doesn't know if his bird is a domestic-bred or an import? Or what if someone claims the bird is a domestic, but you want to be sure?

"Eclectus parrots, domestic-bred, close-banded!" Perhaps you've seen birds wearing a metal band around one leg. If the band is one-piece, if it fits so snugly around the leg that it cannot be slipped on or off, and if it has a letter and number code stamped on it, the chances are good that the bird was born in the United States. The *close* in *close-banded* means that when the bird was about two weeks old, his American breeder slipped a one-piece (closed) ring specially sized for that species over the bird's toes and onto his leg. Some numbers have been registered with a bird club or central registry, so that you can trace the exact date the bird was hatched; these are the best bands of all. Other numbers are used only in the breeder's private breeding program and are not traceable.

Beware of open bands, which are bands wrapped around the bird's leg and closed partway; these can be put on at any time by a breeder or a USDA quarantine station. A USDA band guarantees that the bird is a legal import rather than a smuggled bird, but as we've discussed, this is still not as good as a close-banded domestic.

Should the importation of all birds be prohibited? In Australia it already is: no importing or exporting allowed. The import debate has raged for decades in the United States, but it appears to be coming to an end. U.S. Government regulations on imports are becoming increasingly strict and complex. It is already illegal to import many species, and the government has warned breeders that all importation will stop in the very near future. The beneficial result is that domestic breeding has already increased. It's easier for a pet owner to find a domestic bird than it has ever been, although plenty of imports are still out there.

But should all imported birds be banned simply because they don't make good pets? Or is there another role for them?

Although wild birds imported to the United States are not your best choice for a pet, at least they are alive, while many wild birds in their native countries are often shot or poisoned because they damage crops. Most bird imports come from less-developed countries, where the need for agricultural and timber land is leading native populations to destroy their rain forests. These wild birds are losing their habitat. Without public zoos, wild animal parks, and private owners stepping in to establish breeding programs, these species will become further endangered and may eventually become extinct.

Thus, controlled importation can help keep a species alive where otherwise it would have perished. In many species, the gene pool in captivity is not yet large enough to safely reproduce the species. Importation by private American (and European) breeders—not just captive breeding programs by zoos and wild animal parks—is essential to enlarge the gene pool and continue healthy reproduction. Habitat preservation may be the best way to protect a species, but realistically, it is not going to happen for a very long time. Attempts to work with the Third World on environmental issues are often met with their refusal and/or inability to cooperate because of their own desperate living conditions. Breeding programs—in conjunction with dedicated environmental efforts—are currently the best available option for preservation of a species.

So perhaps the biggest reason why imports should not be kept as pets is this: they can play a more valuable role in breeding programs. Breeder birds are kept with their own kind in a spacious aviary as natural as the breeder can make it. Their freedom and wild lifestyles are curtailed, but they are happier with their own kind than they would be stuck in your living room cage. And they are contributing valuable genes and offspring that will keep the species alive for future generations.

The only negative in buying a domestic-bred bird is price: you'll pay more for a domestic bird. Domestic breeders have to purchase and feed and care for their breeding stock on an ongoing basis. Breeders of parrots also purchase incubators, brooders, and hand-feeding supplies. These increased costs mean increased prices.

HAND-FED

What is hand-feeding? It's the third important term you should look for in your ads: "Eclectus parrots, domestic-bred, close-banded, hand-fed!"

Hand-feeding means that a parrot is taken from his mother when she lays the egg, when he hatches from the egg, or no more than two weeks later. From this moment on, the baby parrot is fed and cared for exclusively by a human being. Hand-fed babies imprint on this human being, looking upon him or her as their own mother. Hand-fed babies trust people so much that sometimes they think they're little people themselves!

You must be careful with this term, though. Some breeders keep hundreds of babies in an outdoor aviary, and their "hand-feeding" may consist of no more than moving along the row of cages, thrusting a tube through the bars of each cage, injecting food into each baby's throat, and moving on to the next cage. This is a useless practice as far as taming goes. If the goal of hand-feeding is to create an incredibly tame and cuddly baby parrot, then the hand-feeding must be carried out quietly and lovingly, and must always be accompanied by soft conversation and a bit of play. It isn't as much the feeding that ensures gentleness but the handling during the feeding. Ask the breeder just how the baby was hand-fed and, if possible, observe how he hand-feeds his other babies.

Some dedicated breeders raise and hand-feed their baby parrots in the living room or family room. Home-raised babies are accustomed to the sights and sounds of a normal home. This is a distinct advantage, as home-raised babies have thus been introduced to all sorts of people, sights, sounds, and situations. They have learned to accept new things with calmness and confidence.

The only disadvantage to a hand-fed baby is that these birds are so devoted to people that they require more time and attention than parent-raised birds. If you're getting a parrot to observe or breed rather than to handle, hand-feeding is not as important. Songbirds, for example, are not hand-fed.

SEXING

Other terms you might run across in classified ads are *surgically sexed* (S/S) or *blood-sexed* or *chromosome-sexed*. The sex of most birds cannot be determined by outward appearance. Different from sexing dogs and cats, you can't just bend over and peek at a bird to determine its sex. Birds have internal sexual anatomy!

You may not be able to tell by size or color, either, and you can't even be sure when two birds sit together and cuddle up to each other, because often it's two males or two females who have bonded. There are a few cage bird species in which the sexes look different, but you can distinguish most parrots only by having your bird "sexed."

You have your choice: surgical sexing means having an avian vet perform an internal abdominal exam with a lighted tube called an endoscope. Since this invasive procedure requires anesthesia—always risky with birds—a newer and better sexing method is to have your vet take a blood feather. Laboratory analysis can then determine your bird's sex by examining the chromosomes in the blood feather. No anesthesia is involved.

Sexing your bird is essential for breeding, but not very important if you only keep it as a pet, unless you just have to know whether your macaw is a Joseph or a Josephine!

5

CONTACTING
SOURCES

You've assembled your list of sources, and you've used your new familiarity of bird terminology to weed out the obviously bad sources. You're ready to start calling the most promising ones. But you're nervous because you don't know what to say.

Let's listen in on a telephone conversation between a reputable breeder of military macaws and a prospective buyer who asks all the right questions. You'll seldom be so lucky as to get one of these perfect breeders, but you'll learn from this conversation the important issues. Then if the breeder doesn't bring them up, you'll be able to do it.

YOU: My name is Kim Vickers and I was given your name by the Willow Veterinary Hospital. I understand you breed military macaws. I wondered if you might have any babies available.

[If the breeder has nothing available, ask for the names of other breeders in the area, and ask if he has any babies planned in the near future. If so, run through as much of this conversation as possible, then ask to visit to decide if his birds would be worth putting down a deposit and waiting.]

BREEDER: I have two babies available, and also an older bird.

YOU: Are they domestic birds? Have they been hand-fed?

BREEDER: The babies are domestic hand-feds; the older bird is an import.

YOU: I'd just be interested in the hand-feds. Have they been handled and played with a lot?

BREEDER: Oh, gosh, yes. These babies have been spoiled and fussed over so much they think they're little people! We raise them right in our living room, you know. They're very friendly and lovable.

YOU: Great! How old are they?

Advantages of a baby bird: He comes to you as a clean slate with no bad habits. You raise him and train him right from scratch. He imprints on you as the most important person in his world. You can watch him grow up.

Disadvantages of a baby bird: He requires much care and supervision, and you can't be sure of how his personality and habits might turn out.

Advantages of an older bird: He's not as delicate as a baby and doesn't require as much adherence to a strict schedule. He may already have had some taming and training. You can better determine what his appearance and personality will be like.

Disadvantages of an older bird: He is bigger and stronger! If he decides to test your leadership, you must be both patient and firm while you establish some control. The bad habits of older birds may be more resistant to change. You missed his fun growing-up years, and you'll never know exactly what experiences he has had or what things he has seen. Also, age is difficult to determine in parrots; a young parrot up to the age of two or three is recognizable, as is an old parrot over fifty, but in between, one guess is often as good as another! Unless you are an experienced owner who knows how to accurately assess the personality of an older bird, you should stick with a baby bird, especially with the larger parrots.

BREEDER: They're a little over four months old.

YOU: Are they completely weaned?

A weaned parrot is eating solid food and no longer needs specially prepared food squirted into his throat. Some breeders recommend that you complete the final phases of hand-feeding and weaning yourself so that the baby bonds strongly to you. Other experts disagree, and so do I. Hand-feeding and weaning can be difficult—if you do something wrong, you could kill your bird. With your first bird, leave hand-feeding and weaning to those who know what they're doing.

BREEDER: Yes, they're eating well on their own.

Military macaws come in only one color, but with some species, you can ask the breeder what color the babies are.

Like most parrots, militaries cannot be sexed by appearance, so there's little use asking the breeder whether his babies are males or females. Breeders do not have their babies surgically sexed. In other species, sex can be ascertained by color, shape of head, behavior, etc., so you *can* ask the breeder whether the babies are males or females. The breeder may call his males *cocks* and his females *hens*.

Which sex makes the better pet? If you find out, write a book about it and then stand back and watch the feathers fly! In some species, males are preferred as pets because they seem to be gentler, friendlier, tamer, and more entertaining. In other species, it's the female who is preferred. In still other species, it doesn't seem to make any difference, and many people never find out because they don't have their bird sexed!

In most species, males are more outgoing than females. They usually are more vocal, which can be a nuisance if they vocalize with screeches and loud whistles, but a thrill if they vocalize primarily by talking.

When male parrots reach sexual maturity, which ranges from one to two years in cockatiels, and four to five years in Amazons, their hormones kick in and they become a bit more difficult to live with. Some individual birds will be worse about this than others, but most parrots show some temperament change during their yearly breeding season. They may become restless, demanding, excitable, and unpredictable. They make strange noises and strut boldly around, admiring themselves in mirrors and trying to breed with everything in sight. If they become aggressive, you may have to keep your handling to a minimum during these times.

Although males are the worst offenders, females are also affected. It's easier to discourage the flirtatious behavior of adult females, but they can still be little wretches. They may even decide to go ahead and lay eggs. Yes, female birds can lay eggs without a male being present. One day they just take it into their head to become a mother, and they busily set about building a nest and depositing eggs. These eggs will not be fertile nor will they hatch, but your bird will be happy nonetheless. She will lay an egg every other day and nestle them under her, nipping anyone who dares approach her. She may incubate her eggs for weeks before giving up. Don't remove the eggs until she loses interest, because she'll just keep on laying more until she reaches the number she thinks she should have!

Chronic egg laying can be a real problem. Since eggshells are made of calcium, a chronic egg layer must receive plenty of calcium so that she can lay firm-shelled eggs. Soft-shelled eggs will be difficult for her to pass—they will bind up inside her. Even with calcium, some birds are prone to this egg binding. People who have dealt with an egg-bound hen or owned a chronic egg layer are often nervous about purchasing another female because of the potential for egg problems.

If you purchase a female who then persists in laying clutch after clutch (bird litters are called clutches), she should be put into a breeding program or given a younger "buddy" bird who might take her mind off laying.

In the species profiles, I note the appreciable differences between males and females. Feel free to ask the breeder for his opinion, but you're probably better off just asking for an assessment of each baby's personality, regardless of its potential sex.

BREEDER: How did you become interested in macaws? Have you owned large parrots before?

Here the breeder is being cautious, trying to find out if you want, say, a cockatoo just because you watched a repeated episode of "Baretta" last night, where the Amazing Fred saved the day. The breeder may ask questions about your children, other pets, living environment, working hours. Don't be offended by his concern. Explain what you know about the temperament, behavior, and requirements of military macaws. Tell the breeder why the military interests you more than other species.

YOU: What price are you asking for the babies?

BREEDER: Twelve hundred dollars.

YOU: I'd like to see them. When would be a good time?

Despite my cautions, you may be seriously considering an older bird, perhaps from a classified ad that you spotted in the newspaper. For an older bird, you'll want to ask the same questions: domestic-bred? hand-fed? age? perhaps sex and color? price? But also include the following questions:

How long have you had him?

Why are you selling him?

What is his personality like—outgoing, energetic, aloof?

Will he bite if I handle him?

What kind of noise does he make?

Does he talk?

Will he talk in front of strangers?

Has he ever plucked his feathers?

Is he a good eater or a picky eater?

What are some of the unusual things that he does?

How many owners has he had?

Avoid birds who have had several owners. Either they have some serious behavioral problem or the repeated changes in environment will have made them too insecure to settle well into still another home.

Assuming that the answers to your questions are satisfactory, let's head out to the breeder's home!

6

ARRIVING AT THE BREEDER'S HOME, AVIARY, OR BIRD STORE

However simple or elaborate the place may be, any area accessible to birds should be clean, safe, and comfortable. Food bowls should contain more than seed: there should be pellets, grains, fruits, and/or vegetables. Perches and nesting boxes should be sturdy, with no jagged edges or protruding nails. Cages should be spacious and not encrusted with muck. Every parrot should have at least one interesting toy in his cage. Trust your instincts; leave if the place looks unsavory. A breeder who doesn't care about his birds' safety is not the breeder for you.

The place will be noisy—boy, will it be noisy! Don't assume that the birds are shrieking because they're upset. They may be delightedly egging each other on! If you've chosen a quiet Bourke's parakeet, you can be grateful that those screaming cockatoos are not going home to your house. If you've chosen a cockatoo . . . oh, well!

Before you look at the babies, walk around and look at the adult birds. They should be clean, fully feathered, and interested in the world around them. An individual bird may be nasty or may have plucked his feathers, but if several of the adults look or act strangely, this is not the breeder from whom you want to buy your bird. As the breeder is showing you around, try to form an impression of him. Is he proud of his birds? Does he speak cheerfully to them? Does he handle them confidently? Do they seem happy to be interacting with him?

Ask the breeder how long he has been involved with birds, and what he likes best and least about your species. An honest breeder should be willing to discuss negative points as well as positive. Remember, you're making a major addition to your life here, especially if you're choosing one of the larger parrots. Don't be embarrassed about double-checking the breeder's expertise; he isn't embarrassed about checking you out as an owner. Both of you are doing the right thing.

Now let's go look at the baby birds you came to see. If you've never seen a baby bird before, you may be envisioning a tiny version of a full-plumage, glorious-color adult bird. Be prepared. Baby birds, especially baby parrots, are odd-looking little things, best described as adorably cute, hysterically funny, and/or hideously ugly.

When I first began looking at baby birds, I ran the gamut of those descriptive phrases. Today I can't imagine how anyone could not be captivated by baby parrots: the fuzzy patchwork of down on their naked breast, their new feathers sticking out like hollow quills, their half-feathered wings that flap awkwardly, their overgrown head with comically rolling eyes, their oversized beak that opens and closes for no apparent reason. "*Urk! Urk!*" they plead.

If you have several babies to choose from, try not to be captivated by the biggest or boldest bird. Don't even handle the birds at first. Stand back from the cage so that your nose isn't pressed against the bars and watch the entire group for as long as possible. You can tell a lot about the individual babies by the way they interact with each other.

Which are outgoing, bossy, noisy? Which are quiet, submissive, gentle? Which ones challenge the others for the choice perching spots? Since most people do best with a bird who is neither too bossy nor too submissive, look for babies who do not initiate trouble, but who do hold their own. Speak and whistle softly to the birds. Which ones are interested and curious? Which are startled or afraid? A nervous baby may grow into a skittish adult.

Let the birds show you their true personality, whatever it may be. Don't try to coax a frightened bird to be brave, trying to convince yourself that you'll be able to "bring him out of his shell." Someday you might want to bring home a nervous bird as a rehabilitation project, but wait until you have more experience with birds.

After you've watched the birds interacting with each other, you'll want to handle and examine each bird individually. (Of course, you don't handle "observation" birds such as songbirds.) Ask the breeder to show you how to pick up a parrot by encouraging them to step onto your hand or finger. A young parrot may be unsteady and may attempt to use his beak to maintain balance—don't look upon this natural reaction as a bite!

You don't really "hold" birds. As human beings, we can breathe with something wrapped around our chest because our diaphragm does the work of moving the air in and out of our lungs. But birds don't have a diaphragm; their breathing depends entirely on the in-and-out movement of their chest. If you hold a bird by wrapping your hand around his chest, he will suffocate. Sometimes you have to catch a small bird by wrapping your hand across his back, with your fingers lightly encircling his throat and abdomen, but most of the time you simply allow him to perch freely on your hand or wrist. That's what *hand-tame* or *finger-tame* means.

If the parrot obviously doesn't want to be handled or attempts to bite you or the breeder, don't consider him any further. You'll sometimes see cages labeled "half-tame" or "semi-tame." In time, these parrots may make fine pets, but I recommend that you look for the tamest bird you can find. However, you can make an exception with budgies, since they're so easy to tame that many breeders don't bother.

With most species that you're hoping to handle, however, the bird should seem eager to be with you, to sit on your hand, to look up into your face when you talk to him, to explore your arm, to nibble at your buttons and jewelry. He should seem curious, attentive, and unafraid.

In the health department, use the following checklist not only before buying a bird but also as a tool in continually reassessing your pet bird's health.

- Are his feathers clean and smooth, or are they fluffed up, ragged-looking, patched with bare spots, or bulging out from some suspicious lump under the skin?
- When he climbs or hops, does he use both legs equally, or does he favor one leg?
- Does he hold both wings naturally against his body, or is one wing held differently from the other?

- Does he have four normal toes on each foot and do his feet and legs have smooth scales, or are there missing toes, deformities, sores, or lumps?
- Is his breast rounded and firm, or does it seem to stick out?
- Is he breathing easily, or is he wheezing, sneezing, or coughing?
- Are the feathers around his nostrils the same color as his other feathers, or are they stained brown or yellow from discharge or vomiting?
- Is his beak smooth, or are there white crusts on it that might signify parasites?
- Are the feathers around his vent (hind end) clean, or are they soiled and sticky?
- Do his droppings consist of a firm green-black bottom part and a soft white upper part, or are they runny and shapeless?
- Does he seem lively and happy? Does he hop or climb or fly around? Does he hold his perch with a firm grip? Does he play with his toys? Does he groom his feathers?
- Does he observe his surroundings with interest, or does he sit in one spot, sometimes even on the floor of the cage, feathers fluffed up, eyes closed, squeaking or wheezing with each breath, sleepy-looking and indifferent to the world?

After you've handled and examined each bird for as long as possible, tell the breeder you'd like to spend some more time watching the birds in their cage. You'll also want to use this time to talk things over with your family and perhaps make a decision.

Don't feel obligated to decide at that very moment. Many thoughtful buyers go home to sleep on their decision, often returning two or three times before they make their final choice. But if you decide that a particular bird seems perfect for your wants, needs, personality, and lifestyle, congratulations! You've made the most informed decision a buyer could ever make, and you should be proud of yourself for all the time and effort you've put into this project.

You should receive a bill of sale that states the date of purchase, price paid, birth date (if known), leg band number, and full description of the bird. You should receive a written health guarantee of a full refund if your veterinarian declares the bird unhealthy within forty-eight hours. Never purchase any bird without this important guarantee. If your bird is a large parrot, you should receive a veterinary health certificate stating that the parrot has passed a CBC (complete blood count), bacterial cultures of the throat and vent, and a psittacosis screen.

You should also receive written instructions on care and feeding, including the type of food the bird is accustomed to eating, how much, and when. If you want to switch the bird to a different type of food, mix the two foods for a while because some birds will literally starve themselves before they'll touch a dish full of unfamiliar food.

If the bird was imported, you should receive a copy of the quarantine certificate.

Be sure you get a receipt for your money.

And you've just bought yourself a fine bird!

On the other hand, if you decide that none of these particular birds is right for you, say politely: "These are really nice birds, but we don't see exactly what we're looking for right now. Thank you for showing them to us."

I know you're disappointed, but you'd be more disappointed if you took home the wrong bird just because you wanted to buy something. Reflect on everything that this valuable first experience has taught you. Call the next source on your list. Take your time. The search will be worth it.

Step Four

CARING FOR
YOUR NEW BIRD

7

PREPARING THE CAGE AND ACCESSORIES

Should you bring your bird home the moment you buy him, and what should you have prepared for your new pet?

Too many people stroll into the pet shop and impulsively buy a parakeet, a cage, some toys, and some seeds. In Chapter 1, when I discussed the true cost of a bird plus equipment, I mentioned some children who begged their father for a ten-dollar parakeet. Let's look at what typically happens when you buy a bird the way they did.

The happy family drives home with their frightened bird bouncing around in his cardboard box. Once home, the bird cowers, waiting while the family dashes around looking for a good spot for the cage. With mounting anticipation, they rip open the shrink-wrapped packages of toys and argue about how to arrange the perches and the ladders and the bells and the rings. They stuff everything into the cage so that there is barely room for the bird.

They fill the food dish to the brim with new seeds. Nobody can seem to locate last night's newspaper to line the bottom of the cage.

Finally, they push the parakeet into his new castle and wait excitedly for him to do something: to explore his new toys, to gobble his new seed, to hang upside down from his new perches, perhaps even to say, "Hey, thanks! This is great!"

The parakeet, meanwhile, has scrambled to the highest and farthest corner of the cage. There he clings, terrified, while the family stares in dismay. When the oldest girl reaches in to pet him, he pecks at her finger. "Boy, we sure picked a lulu!" says the father in disgust. "Let's turn on the TV and watch something else."

What a disaster!

Let's find a much better way to do things. You already chose a suitable species, you found an excellent breeder or bird store, and you purchased a tame and healthy bird. Now you need to choose and prepare his cage, playground, toys, and food so that everything will be waiting for your bird when you bring him home.

First the housing, then the birds.

If you were sure all along that you wanted a certain species, you might even have purchased and prepared the cage and equipment before you went to the breeder. That way, you could have brought your bird home the same day you bought him. But after reading the profiles, looking at color photos, and seeing some birds up close, you might have been torn between two or three species. You might not have made your final decision until you were actually handling the different birds, and if you were trying to decide between a thirty-inch macaw and a fifteen-inch dwarf macaw, you would not have been able to purchase the cage ahead of time.

WHERE TO PLACE THE CAGE

Before you even consider what type of cage to buy, you should look around your home and decide where you are going to put it.

When new owners learn that sunlight, an easy-clean floor, and an active environment are important for birds, they immediately think of the kitchen. It's usually a cheerful room with bright light coming in the windows, people bustling in and out and sharing two or three meals a day, and a smooth vinyl or tile floor. It's perfect!

No, it isn't. It's the most dangerous room in the house to keep your bird. The kitchen is chock-full of cooking odors and cleaning fumes that can kill your bird. Most of us cook with pots and pans that have a nonstick coating such as Teflon, Silverstone, or Supra. Did you know that if you accidentally leave one of those pans on the fire and it overheats, it will release a poisonous gas that will kill your bird?

Remember when miners brought caged canaries into the mine shafts with them? Birds are so sensitive to fumes that they served as an early warning of danger. When a canary suddenly keeled over, it meant that dangerous gases were seeping into the mine. In exactly the same way you may lose your bird if you use nonstick cookware. If you're very, very stubborn and very, very reluctant to give up this convenience, you must do *all* of the following to safeguard your bird every time you use a nonstick pan:

1. Shift the cage to the farthest room away from the kitchen.

2. Turn on the stove fan to draw out the fumes.

3. Open the kitchen window.

Imagine how difficult this third step is going to be if you live where the temperature drops below freezing in winter, not to mention that now you're creating a cold draft for your bird! Don't you think it would be easier and safer just to replace the pans? And while you're at it, replace your clothes iron or curling iron if either has a nonstick coating.

The tragedies that nonstick coatings have caused are very real. This is not a simple caution, but a powerful warning. *Bird Talk* magazine is constantly running articles on this subject, and yet they still print anguished letters from owners who lost their beloved birds because they failed to take the necessary precautions. Anyone who takes on the responsibility of a pet bird must protect it from this most deadly hazard of our modern homes.

Even if you don't use nonstick coatings, the kitchen is not a very good place to keep your bird. There will always be smoke and cooking fumes, and the odors of cleaning compounds under the sink. The only exception might be if part of your kitchen, such as a breakfast nook, is clearly separated from the cooking area and you use your stove fan or ceiling fan a lot and keep your windows and doors open much of the time.

Let's look at the other rooms in your house and find out how they're all unsuited to birds in some way! (Yes, finding a room that's safe and comfortable for the bird and convenient for you can be hard to do!)

If you put the cage in your bedroom, your sleep may be disturbed. Most birds sleep quietly all night, but they may wake up earlier than you'd like. In addition, bedrooms are usually isolated so that your bird wouldn't be able to see anything going on in the rest of the house. He wouldn't receive enough attention. And you're likely to use deodorant and hair sprays in there, both of which are risky around birds.

A walk-in closet is too isolated, with no access to natural light and fresh air. So is a storage room, attic, or basement. The garage is too drafty, too dark, and too full of exhaust, paint, and insecticide fumes. Birds require at least twelve hours of reliable light every day.

How about a busy hallway? Although you're looking for a location with activity, where your bird will feel like a family participant, don't overdo it! A narrow hallway where people rush back and forth within a few inches of the cage would soon make a nervous wreck out of your bird, perhaps turning him into a defensive nipper.

The rooms that usually work best for birds are the living room, dining room, and family room. Once you've chosen the right room, you need to choose the right spot in that room. Don't place the cage beside the entrance-way or in the center of the room where the bird will be exposed on all sides while people run at him from every direction. Place it in or near one of the corners so that he feels secure. If you have a choice of corners, the one nearest the window is best. Birds love to look outdoors and they love sunlight.

In fact, sunlight is so important to your bird that if his cage will not be receiving some sun for a few hours every day, you should be able to carry or roll the cage to such a location. An alternative is to provide an ultraviolet light such as Vita-Lite; you can pick these up at a flower shop or hardware store.

But remember that access to sun demands equal access to shade. Since the sun moves in the sky, what was shade when you left your bird can become sun very quickly. Birds are very susceptible to over-heating. If your bird flattens the feathers of his wings and holds the wings away from his body, he is too warm. Bring him into an air-conditioned room and use a plant mister to soak him with cool water. Offer fresh water to drink and encourage him to soak his belly in a shallow dish of water. However, if the bird is also panting and looking glassy-eyed, the condition has progressed to heatstroke. To prevent brain dam-age and death, head immediately to the vet, ideally in an air-conditioned car.

Thus, you must place the bird's cage, whether permanently or temporarily, so that some part of it remains in shade at all times. Also check that the window is securely attached to the frame or weather-stripped so that there is no draft. Draft is a deadly enemy of birds—they can tolerate extreme cold much more easily than the slightest draft. Check that the cage will not receive a draft from any exterior door, and that no air blows on the cage from a heating register or air-conditioning vent.

One final caution about windows: if you live in a busy neighborhood or high-crime area and own an expensive or unusual-looking bird, make sure the cage is hidden from passersby who might see your bird as a potential money-maker. Blinds are a good way to let your bird see out without letting anyone else see in.

Once you've chosen a corner based on natural light and freedom from drafts, check for a few more things. The television or stereo shouldn't be right beside the cage, especially if your kids love MTV. Electrical wires, curtains, plants, and drawstrings for drapes and blinds should not be within reach of curious beaks.

Look at the walls around the cage and the flooring under the cage. In an earlier chapter I explained that carpeted rooms are not very practical for bird keeping, so naturally your living room, dining room, and family room are carpeted, right? And you probably have lovely wallpaper that cost a pretty penny. If you're bringing home a messy bird like a mynah or a large parrot, cover the wallpaper around the cage with clear sheeting. No, it won't look very glamorous, but it will protect the walls from splattered fruit and droppings.

Whether you're bringing home a parrot or a canary, you should also cover the carpeting under the cage with a vinyl chair mat, a tablecloth, or even a shower curtain. All birds enjoy rooting through the food bowl to find the best food, which they believe is on the very bottom, while the yucky top layer is cheerfully tossed out of the cage. It's very difficult to vacuum up seed hulls, pellets, cucumber seeds, cracker grains, and feathers out of deep pile carpeting, so put down that easy-care pad—and if it's near Christmas, drop a hint that you'd like Santa to bring you a Dustbuster! The pad is important, too, for cleaning the cage. Water will inevitably drip onto the floor while you're scrubbing encrusted droppings off the cage bars, and little bits of "stuff" will scatter onto the floor every time you change the newspapers.

If birds love sunlight and the outdoors, could you keep the cage outdoors? Some people do keep their birds on a patio or sun porch, either in a regular cage or in a small aviary. This is fine when the climate is mild, the shade and sunlight are equal, and the cage is protected from rain, insects, theft, and other animals by a fence or shrubbery. Songbirds especially seem to appreciate these quiet locations.

BUYING THE RIGHT CAGE

It does little good to choose a wonderful bird from an excellent breeder and then house him in a rotten cage. If the cage is improper, your wonderful bird will become ill, shriek himself hoarse, beat his wings against the bars, pluck his feathers, or wither away and die. The larger parrots may resort to bizarre bobbing or swaying head motions that make them look drunk.

Never underestimate how much space a bird needs. No matter how big it seems, the cage you're looking at is not too large for your bird—if anything, it's probably too small. Remember that the space we offer birds is never more than a poor substitute for the open spaces that nature provided.

Don't be frightened away by the high prices of bigger cages. Don't be so short-sighted as to spend a thousand dollars on a macaw and then stick him in a one hundred dollar cage because you were too cheap to spend three hundred. Over the next fifty years, all the behavioral problems you're going to see will never be worth the two hundred bucks you saved.

If you're ever going to splurge for anything in your bird's lifetime, splurge on the cage. Make it extremely roomy, even if you have to overextend yourself. In fifty years, when your wonderful bird is still healthy and happy, that extra two hundred dollars will seem like peanuts.

How big is big enough? In most species profiles, I recommend a minimum size cage, but also ask the breeder or bird store owner—then try to get at least one size larger! At the very least, your bird should be able to fully stretch and flap both wings without touching the sides of the cage.

To walk into a bird cage showroom, with all those dazzling homes of all shapes, sizes, and colors, you'd never think that it would be so difficult to find a good cage. Look, there's a cage shaped like a Conestoga wagon!

But your problem won't be choosing among all those cages. Rather, it will be finding even one cage that's suitable. Most of those ornate cages are nice to look at on the outside, but unsuitable from the more important inside, where the bird must live.

First, many cages are just too darned small. You'll find cages labeled for parakeets or cockatiels that would barely allow your bird to hop from perch to perch. These are prisons, not comfortable homes.

Second, many cages are made from impractical materials. Wrought iron is difficult to clean because of its curly design. Oriental bamboo and wicker are equally difficult to clean, tend to warp when wet, and any self-respecting parrot will chew them to ribbons within a week.

Third, many cages are poorly shaped. Rounded cages cut down on interior room and sometimes make birds nervous. Apparently the rounded top appears to fold in on the bird. Also stay away from cages shaped like tall towers. In a small apartment, these might seem like efficient space-savers, but large birds cannot spread their wings in these cages, and small birds are not helicopters—they do not fly vertically.

So what should you be looking for? Roominess, first and foremost. Then a simple rectangular shape, or a cage that slopes outward at the bottom (or comes with a flared cage apron) to help keep much of the mess inside the cage. Finally, simple chrome, brass, or baked enamel finishes are sturdy and easy to clean.

If you're on a budget, you can sometimes find used bird cages at garage sales and through newspaper classifieds, but make sure the cage is not an older or cheap imported model painted with a lead finish. Also find out what happened to the bird who used to live inside the cage; did he die of a contagious disease? Be prepared to heavily disinfect used cages before you put your new bird inside.

Next, examine the cage bars. The thickness (or gauge) of each bar depends on the type of bird you're getting. The large parrots with their powerful beaks need the heaviest bars and the sturdiest welds available. If the bars "give" when you squeeze them with one hand, they are not strong enough for a macaw or cockatoo.

Since parrots like to climb, it would be ideal if most of the bars were horizontal rather than vertical, but you'll have to search hard for this feature and probably settle for just a couple of horizontal bars. Most parrots don't have a problem with this; they hook their feet on and scramble right up.

The bars should be spaced close enough so that your bird cannot get his head stuck between them. Many birds die each year because they were able to wedge their heads through the bars and then panicked and broke their necks. For a songbird or budgie, the bars should be no more than three-eighths of an inch apart; for a cockatiel or conure, no more than one-half inch apart; for larger parrots, no more than one inch apart. Take the cages down and compare them. Also check the corners and roof of the cage: the bars should not become narrower or form a triangle where your bird could get stuck.

Next, examine the cage doors. There should be one main door and two smaller doors for easy access to food and water dishes. Without access doors, you have to stick your hand in the cage every time you want to feed your bird or change his water. Pet sitters will also appreciate access doors.

The main door should not slide up and down like a guillotine. Birds like to stick their beaks under guillotine doors and try to raise them and squeeze under them. Even worse than your bird escaping, this type of door could suddenly fall on your bird's neck. Instead, the door should be hinged on the side or bottom, and if the hinge is spring-loaded so that it closes automatically, remove the spring so that the door can't snap shut on your bird. The main door opening should be large enough for you to easily access the entire interior of the cage. These features seem so obvious that you'd think cage makers would know all about them, but many of the cages you'll see on the market have guillotine, spring-loaded, or absurdly tiny doors!

Finally, examine the bottom portion of the cage. The floor should extend several inches up the sides of the cage to help keep the mess inside. There should be a slide-out tray for easy cleaning. Sometimes a grate separates the bird from the newspapers in the slide-out tray. If the grate is removable, many owners do just that. Theoretically the grate is useful because the droppings fall through onto the tray, and so the bird can't dirty himself by hopping through them. But many owners remove the grate because it becomes clogged with droppings and is a nuisance to clean.

If you're not getting a freestanding parrot cage, you'll also need a stand to place the cage on. You can buy a ready-made stand or use a wide sturdy end table, and the height should be such that the bird lives at your eye level or below. Make sure that the stand cannot be tipped over easily; if you live in earthquake country, consider bolting or otherwise securing the cage to the widest-legged table you can find.

An Aviary or Bird Room?

If you've decided to keep songbirds or a group of small parrots such as budgies or lovebirds, you might consider an indoor aviary rather than a cage. An aviary need not be longer than six feet nor deeper than two feet. It generally stands floor to ceiling, or nearly so. You can buy small ready-made aviaries or build one yourself.

An indoor aviary can be made of wood and wire, or it can be glass-fronted with solid rear and side walls. Place it in one corner of the room and furnish it with live branches and potted plants. Install Vita-Lites in the top portion and cover the floor with sand and pine needles. Consider covering the back and side walls with a beautiful nature or landscape scene. You might even put rollers or wheels on it so that you can move it around to take advantage of natural sunlight.

You can also devote an entire room to your bird. This would require mesh screens over the windows and a wire-mesh entrance hall just inside the door so that the birds couldn't fly through the rest of the house every time you opened the door to enter the bird room.

Indoor aviaries and bird rooms increase life expectancy because your birds receive plenty of exercise in a natural environment where they feel protected. When well built and tastefully decorated, these housing alternatives also make a spectacular addition to your home, and provide an endless conversation topic for you and your guests.

Buying the Right Accessories for the Cage

Once you've picked out your bird's house, you'll need to furnish it so that it truly becomes a home.

First, you'll need perches. One or two may come with the cage, but if they're slippery plastic, pitch them into the deepest wastebasket you can find. You're supposed to be furnishing the cage to resemble your bird's natural habitat. Very few trees have plastic branches.

Simple wooden dowels are acceptable, but even these are unnatural compared to the tree branches that wild birds are privileged to climb around on. If you spend just a few minutes scouting around your yard or a nearby park or woods, you'll probably find several branches that will make fantastic furniture. Make sure they haven't been sprayed with pesticides, leave the bark on, scrub them with hot water, and let them dry before attaching them to the cage with strong rope or wire. Their different sizes and shapes mean that your bird's feet will get a healthy workout. He will need to adjust his grip on the different branches just as he would in nature. Each perch should be thick enough that his toes cannot grip all the way around.

Since chewing is one of the favorite hobbies of a parrot, they enjoy chewing on their perches, so the perches will have to be replaced periodically. If you live in the middle of the desert and can't find tree branches, your bird store or pet shop may offer thick branches of manzanita wood.

The number and placement of the perches requires some thought. Don't put in so many that your songbird has no room to fly and your parrot has no room to play. Don't place perches over food and water dishes, or over other perches—for obvious soiling reasons. Don't place perches where the bird's head or tail would rub against the cage bars when he sits on the perch.

In one corner of the cage, you may also want to offer a flat platform for your bird to stand on.

You're saving money by using natural branches as perches. Another freebie furnishing can be the lining paper you use in the slide-out tray. You can buy special bird paper, but most bird owners just use brown grocery bags that

169

have been cut to fit, or even more commonly newspaper. There's always the chance that your bird could turn out to be a paper swallower and the ink in the newsprint could cause digestive problems, but most owners put the paper in there anyway, and have no problems. Use black-and-white sheets only—the color process contains chemical remnants that could really bother your bird. Don't use kitty litter; this could block up your bird's respiratory tract.

With some species, you might want to add a small nesting box so that your bird has a private place to sleep, and to chew to shreds. You can buy a nesting box, you can build one out of wood, or you can just throw a cardboard box in there and replace it periodically!

Food and water dishes may come with the cage, you may have to buy them, or you might find something suitable in your cupboard. They should be wide rather than deep, because birds root around in deep dishes and end up wasting half the food. They should be nontippable, nonchewable, and easy to clean. For songbirds, you can buy a food dish with a hood to help keep the seed in the dish, but never buy a dish like this for parrots, including budgies. For some reason, many parrots would starve to death rather than put their heads under a hood.

With the exception of a few species such as budgies, most birds drink by filling their beaks with water, raising their head, and letting the water run down their throat. Thus, the water dish must be deep enough to allow them to dip their bills in.

For cleaning the cage bars, you should gather a supply of sandpaper and an old toothbrush or scrub brush. You can also buy special perch scrapers. When you clean the cage, use very hot water with no cleansers or detergents. You can either place your bird on his playground at this time or keep him in a box.

You won't need a cover for the cage unless your bird will be kept in a very bright or active room where he wouldn't be able to get ten to twelve hours sleep every night. Birds must have this amount of sleep to stay healthy.

Finally, if you've chosen a parrot, he will need playthings—lots of heavy-duty, interesting, chewable playthings. Songbirds seldom play with toys, but they are essential for parrots, providing stimulation, challenge, and exercise. Parrots without toys are bored parrots, and bored parrots shriek, bite, and pluck their feathers.

High-quality toys are made of hardwood, vegetable-tanned leather, non-toxic beads, tightly linked chain, heavy acrylic, and/or natural cotton, sisal, or jute rope. Stroll through your bird store or thumb through *Bird Talk* magazine, and you'll discover a mind-boggling array of safe, colorful, heavy-duty chewables for your eager parrot to start working on.

If you're short on funds, you can also make chewable toys. Bore holes through nontoxic hardwood (such as children's building blocks) and string the wood onto undyed rawhide shoelaces. Rummage through your attic for old-fashioned wooden clothespins—the kind without springs; parrots love to hold these in their toes and gnaw on them. When shopping, pick up some corn on the cob—your parrot gets a healthy meal to boot! If your dog doesn't like his Nylabone, offer it to your parrot, or offer an empty paper towel roll or washed pine cone.

But don't jam all the toys into the cage at once. To maintain your parrot's interest and use your space efficiently, rotate the toys. Or give your parrot a choice: some parrots love to rummage through an undyed woven basket that contains several toys for them to play with and discard as the mood strikes them.

Never offer plastic pet-shop toys to anything larger than a budgie, lovebird, or cockatiel. Medium to large parrots will quickly crack those toys and cut themselves. The owners of large parrots often spend years searching for toys that are heavy-duty enough to withstand the awesome power of these big-beaked birds.

If you hang any toy in the cage, be sure it is on a short, thick rope or chain. A long thin string can strangle your bird. To clamp toys to the cage bars, use wooden clothespins or special spring clips found in pet supply stores.

Remember that parrots are suspicious of new things, so new toys may not be accepted right away. Don't be dismayed to see your wonderful $24.95 toy hanging idly in the corner of the cage for days; sooner or later, your parrot will probably approach it and give it a cautious try.

One final recommendation for freebie entertainment: turn on the radio, stereo, or television whenever you go out. Birds love music and most have definite tastes. Some enjoy easy listening or soft classical; they'll dance or sing or just sit quietly and listen to a whole turntable of Beethoven symphonies. Others are staunch fans of The Grateful Dead.

BUYING OR BUILDING THE RIGHT PLAYGROUND

Along with the toys in their cage, most parrots will need a separate playground, jungle gym, and/or T-stand. You may have seen old movies where large parrots were chained to their perch, but you should never do this. If your bird became frightened and tried to fly, he could severely injure his chained leg.

There are many excellent commercial playgrounds to choose from, but if they seem too expensive and/or you're a handy person, you could build your own. Examine as many commercial models as you can for ideas, then use traditional hardwood and branches to create your own design. For smaller birds such as budgies, a playground usually consists of a large wooden tray, to which is mounted a variety of ladders and swings. You place the playground on a nearby table and the budgies both run around the tray and play on the toys.

The playground of larger birds may be a similar design on a larger scale, or it may be more of a tree design or jungle gym. This consists of a weighted base that rests on the floor, a six- or seven-foot center pole, and a variety of wooden dowels poking through the center pole. Parrots clamber enthusiastically across the dowels and play with heavy-duty chew toys and climbing ropes. *Bird Talk* magazine sometimes runs articles on building unusual playgrounds that will pique your parrot's interest.

Since your parrot should be placed on his playground at least once a day, it should be set up close to the cage. Of course, your parrot will be out of his cage when he is on his playground. If you're worried about him wandering through your house and leaving droppings everywhere, you can try to housebreak him. Yes, some parrots (the larger ones, especially) can be housebroken. The difficulty lies in the rapid and continuous digestion of birds; they are constantly forming and releasing new wastes. Also, birds are not den animals like dogs and cats, so they have no natural instincts to keep their quarters clean. They simply go to the bathroom whenever they feel the urge, no matter where they are.

But if you have a parrot who gives some warning that he is about to produce a dropping, such as shifting a certain way or making a certain sound, try quickly picking him up and holding him over the papers you want used. Use an appropriate phrase such as "Go potty!" and add lots of praise when he performs. Eventually you may end up with a reasonably housebroken bird who goes to the papers of his own accord. One polite Amazon informs his owner as he leaves the playground: "Gotta go! Be right back!"

Worried about your parrot flying around loose? He won't if you keep his wing feathers trimmed short. Indeed, it is irresponsible to allow your bird to wear his wing fingers naturally long and fly freely around your house. There are too many dangers in the average household, and many of them are so innocent-looking that you're bound to forget something. You'll leave a window cracked or your child will open the screen door to dash in to the bathroom, and your bird will zoom through and be gone. You'll forget to remove just one slippery chair and that will be where your bird will land, and slip and break a leg. You'll forget to block off just one poisonous plant, and that will be the one nibbled on when you're not looking.

The number of normal household items that are dangerous to birds boggles the mind: cosmetics such as your nail polish and deodorant stick, the crayons and markers that have somehow crawled under the sofa, coins and jewelry that are irresistibly shiny, simple medicines such as the cough syrup your kids spilled on the sink, the fabric softener you dripped in the laundry room, the antifreeze stain on your work gloves, all painting and cleaning products, the batteries for your son's Monster Truck, the lovely antiques that contain poisonous lead or tiffany, the foil from the liquor bottles left on the coffee table, Sheetrock, suntan lotion, mothballs, house plants, tipsy appliances such as your mixer, waxed furniture, electrical wires, stove burners, radiators, sewing and knitting needles, vases that a bird can stick his head into, open toilets, and every bottle and aerosol can that you know you're supposed to keep under your sink but which was somehow left out.

Birds are curious creatures—they get into everything. Even your floor can harm your bird. If you don't step on him, the flooring that he nibbles at may contain lead. So clip, clip, clip, and constantly check, check, check to be sure those wing feathers are still short, because they grow back every few months. Clipping does not hurt your parrot in the slightest. You're not really clipping the wings; you're only clipping the ends off seven or eight feathers, and feathers have no nerves. Your bird may dislike being restrained for the trimming procedure, but he doesn't feel the actual trimming, and thirty seconds of ticked-off parrot is a minuscule price to pay for months of safety.

A bird store will trim your bird's wings for a few dollars, while a vet will charge quite a bit more. Make sure the store clips both wings, never just one side. Some bird stores still recommend this one-side-only practice, saying "It throws him off balance so he can't fly very far." It sure does—only he's so unbalanced that when he tries to fly he often crashes and injures himself. If a bird store recommends this, find a more enlightened store.

Even with clipped wings, some birds can fly enough to make it across your room. Until your bird shows you that he can't fly enough to hurt himself, you should take precautions whenever he is on his playground. Close all blinds, drapes, shades, and shutters, or he may fly into the glass windows thinking they're open spaces. For the same reason, cover your mirrors. Close and lock all doors against unexpected visitors. Even a half-open door leading to another room is an invitation for a bird to fly to the top of the door; if the door happens to swing shut, your bird could be crushed. Remove other pets, toddlers, toxic houseplants, and cacti. Turn off ceiling fans, stove burners, and electrical appliances. And gentlemen, if ever there was an incentive to put down the toilet seat, the prospect of a drowned bird should do it.

BUYING THE RIGHT FOODS

Fortunately, the days are long gone when responsible owners simply poured seeds into their bird's food dish every couple of days. Seeds supply carbohydrates, but not the proteins and vitamins that birds need. Since wild birds choose from a veritable smorgasbord of grasses, seeds, shoots, and berries, it's your responsibility to offer your pet bird just as wide a variety. Without a balanced diet your bird will become ill and its life will be shortened.

Instead of seeds, offer a pelleted diet such as Nutri-Berries or Roudybush. Pellets are extremely nutritious and chock-full of everything your bird needs to stay healthy and happy. You can still offer seeds, but use them more as a snack. Pour some seed into an airtight container and store it at room temperature because birds don't like cold foods. Store the bulk of the seed in your refrigerator to keep it fresh. Add a little of the room-temperature seed to his food dish every afternoon. Make sure there aren't too many sunflower seeds in the mixture; parrots love these so much they'll gorge themselves and ignore everything else!

Note: If your new bird is accustomed to only seeds, feed an equal mixture of pellets and seeds for a while, then gradually add more pellets and fewer seeds.

As far as how many pellets to feed, you have to play it by ear. Fill the bowl halfway and see how much your bird leaves. You'll soon learn how much he will eat at a single sitting, how much he picks during the day, and when you will need to refill. Try to keep your bird on the slim side. Obesity causes lethargy and health problems.

Make sure you know the true amount of food in your bird's dish. When birds eat seeds, for example, they crack open the hull, pull out the kernel, and drop the hull back into the dish. At first glance a dish full of split seed hulls can look like a dish full of food. Don't make this mistake. Blow off or throw away the used hulls so that you can see what's really left. And always keep some food in your bird's dish at all times; small birds could die if deprived of food for even half a day.

Birds who are eating a nutritious pellet diet still require variety. Every day, offer several foods from this list: whole wheat bread or crackers, cooked brown rice, broccoli, spinach, lima or kidney beans, green beans, lettuce, grated carrot, cucumber, parsley, squash, sweet potato, pumpkin, apple, banana, grapes, berries, oranges, pears, hard-boiled or scrambled egg, figs, dates, raisins, peanuts, and a very small amount of yogurt and cottage cheese. Rinse fruits and vegetables thoroughly before offering them.

Most foods that are good for you are good for your bird, including pizza! However, there are some foods that should never be offered to birds: avocado, chocolate, and heavily greased or heavily salted foods.

When it comes to fresh foods, birds have definite likes and dislikes, so you must keep experimenting until you find a selection that your particular bird will accept. Songbirds and small parrots such as budgies are especially fussy, and it can sometimes be difficult to get them to eat any fresh foods. Keep trying. Offer fresh foods in a separate dish, change the foods frequently, and clean the dish often. Try clipping some fresh foods to the cage bars.

A varied diet is not only important for proper nutrition but also a good habit that your bird should develop. In an emergency, you might find yourself out of his accustomed food and he could starve in refusing to accept substitutes. During an illness, flexible birds may be able to keep up their strength by picking at different foods, while rigid birds might refuse everything and die.

There are three other foods you'll want to clip to the cage bars: millet sprays, which provide exercise and amusement as he pries the seeds off; a mineral block; and a cuttlebone, which contains calcium and helps keep beaks short and sharp. Since your bird's beak grows constantly, he can only wear it down by cracking seeds, rubbing it against a perch, or gnawing at toys and cuttlebones. A beak that grows too long must be professionally trimmed.

At the pet supply shop, you might see vitamins that can be added to your bird's water. If your bird is eating a pelleted diet along with fresh foods, he is getting all the vitamins he needs, so don't waste your money. However, if he is a fussy eater who refuses fresh foods, you should sprinkle powdered vitamins, such as Avian Plus, on his pellets and seeds several times a week. Don't buy the vitamins that must be added to your bird's water; they encourage the growth of bacteria and make the water taste bad.

At the pet shop you might also see grit, a grainy mixture that supposedly helps your bird grind up his food. Again, don't waste your money. Many veterinarians strongly advise against grit because it can become impacted in the bird's digestive system and create serious health problems.

An increasing number of bird owners, concerned about chemicals in city tap water, are offering bottled water or filtered tap water to their birds.

Compared to other pets, birds drink very little water, especially Australian birds. Budgies drink less than a teaspoon a day. However, when your bird does need water, he really needs it, so his bowl must be kept filled with fresh water. Some birds won't touch a water bowl with a piece of newspaper or muck floating in it.

8

BRINGING YOUR BIRD HOME

I know you're excited about the spacious and shiny cage that will be your bird's new home, but don't bring it along when you go to pick him up. He will feel so exposed that he will scramble up the bars to the highest corner, and then fall off because he won't be able to predict the starts and stops and turns of your car. Instead, transport him in a snug carrier with solid sides. For small birds, cardboard boxes with punched air holes will do nicely, while larger birds do well in a cardboard cat carrier or a small solid-sided dog crate with a wire door.

On a hot summer day, turn on the air-conditioning, and on a cold winter day, turn on the heat, but aim the vents away from the cage. Play the radio softly, and occasionally speak to the bird. Never be so foolish as to ride with your new bird in your arms or on your lap! This is dangerous, and certainly doesn't get your responsible ownership history off to a good start.

Once home, place the bird gently into his new cage, or press the carrier door against the cage door and encourage him to go in of his own accord. Make sure he has fresh water and the same kind of food that he is accustomed to eating. This is not the time to change food. Then leave the bird alone. Occasionally approach his cage and speak pleasantly to him, but give him time to settle in. Don't handle him and don't let your children touch him. Remember that birds react badly to any change in environment.

If you have another bird in your home, it is imperative to keep your new bird in a separate cage in a separate room for thirty days. During that time, check both birds daily for signs of illness. I know this waiting time is difficult, especially if you purchased the new bird as a companion for your other bird. You're anxious to see how they'll interact. But you could lose your precious first bird if the new one has some illness that hasn't yet shown itself.

When should you bring your new bird to the vet for a health check? Some experts recommend that you stop off at the vet's on the way home from the seller. Then you won't have to get your bird all the way home and settled in his new cage, only to have to coax him back out tomorrow for another unsettling car ride.

This sounds perfect in theory, but in practice, unless you're so organized that you called for a veterinary appointment a couple of days in advance, coordinated your pick-up time at the seller, and then actually managed to meet that schedule, it may not work. Or the seller may live in the opposite direction from the veterinary hospital, or you may want to pick up your bird at a time that's convenient for *you*, but not for your vet.

To be honest, few buyers of songbirds and small parrots such as budgies take their birds to the vet at all. These birds are so easy to obtain and so inexpensive that an additional thirty dollars for the vet to examine a lively, healthy looking bird often seems a waste of time and money. The vet will look for the same signs of poor health that you have already screened for at the breeder's. If you want more in-depth blood tests or cultures, you're facing even more expense. You may want to rely upon your vet's recommendation of tests to perform, but it's really up to you. Bird fanciers seem divided in their opinion of just how much testing is enough and how much is too much, especially for smaller birds.

Large parrots should come with a veterinary certificate showing that they've already been examined at least once, but a second trip to your vet confirming the bird's good health should be done within the time period of the health guarantee. This also allows the vet to become acquainted with your new bird.

≈　　≈　　≈

After your bird has settled into your home—meaning that he is eating well, grooming, and showing interest when you approach his cage—you can begin to hand-tame if you are planning to do so. Hand-raised birds will already be eager to interact with you, of course, which is why you should make every effort to purchase them. Refer to your bird behavior books and *Bird Talk* articles for the best methods to train and tame your bird.

9

BEHAVIORAL PROBLEMS

Songbirds seldom show behavioral problems, but parrots do. The most common parrot behavioral problems are screaming, feather plucking, and biting. You've just finished reading that sentence, and now you're smiling at your adorable blue-and-gold macaw and shaking your head with an indulgent, "This chapter is for other people—my baby is an angel!"

But the best way to solve a behavioral problem is to prevent it from happening, and the best way to prevent it is to keep your parrot's life stress-free, while taking firm charge of that life. You've provided the roomy cage, the light and sunshine, the varied diet, the interesting toys and playtime, a reasonably predictable schedule, and plenty of companionship. Now you must be the leader of your household.

Parrots use body posture, facial expression, and voice to communicate with each other and with you. Sadly, you may not even recognize what your bird is trying to say. You must read articles on bird behavior if you are to understand your parrot and establish yourself as leader. If your parrot feels that you are uncertain or afraid, or if you allow him to dominate you, you will see a plethora of behavioral problems.

In a multi-owner household where one person is the leader, the bird may test the other person. "Our sulphur-crested cockatoo is fine with me, but not with my husband!" Or vice versa. Birds always seem to nip guests who don't like them or who are afraid of them. They pick up the guest's uncertainty and test to see if they can dominate. Sometimes it's done playfully, sometimes seriously. Parrots like to find out who's who.

If you're concerned that you'll have to abuse your bird to show who's boss, put that thought far from your mind. You're aiming for psychological rather than physical superiority. Convince the baby parrot with a confident voice and attitude that you are in charge, that you will make all the decisions, and that you have everything under control; that way, the bird is less likely to challenge you as an adult.

Teach your parrot the "Up!" command, which means that he will climb onto your finger or wrist when you hold your hand in front of his legs; even climbing onto a stick will do, if you don't want to (or can't) hold him on your hand or arm. Once he is on your hand or arm, don't allow him to climb onto your shoulder or across the back of your neck where he can easily avoid your groping hands.

Place his cage so that he cannot look down on you. In fact, if your bird is already too dominant, some behaviorists recommend lowering the cage to waist level (or blocking off the upper portion of a freestanding cage), or even housing the bird on the floor for a while so that the bird must look up to see an approaching person's eyes. This is psychological dominance. It doesn't seem like much to you, but it means a lot to a pushy parrot.

Similarly, playgrounds and jungle gyms should be kept low. Try to move the playground to different areas of the room, or even to other rooms, so that your bird doesn't become too territorial or possessive of what is "his."

Ideally, a parrot should be handled by all members of the family so that he doesn't bond too strongly to one member. He should also spend some time by himself so that he doesn't become overly dependent on human companion-ship. Don't talk to him or tickle or pick him up every time you walk by his cage. He must learn how to entertain himself: you don't want to become a slave to a bossy bird.

How do you handle screaming? Your first impulse is to lock your screaming bird in a back room where you can't hear him! But screamers should be moved closer into the family, not isolated further.

Your bird may be screaming because he is angry, happy, jealous, bored, or simply saying hello. He may be screaming because you are rewarding him with an exciting "energy response." Do you rush toward his cage, screw your face into a disapproving frown, shake your finger, and shout to be quiet? What an exciting show this is for your bird! He will be delighted to repeat this game over and over. Screamers often manipulate their owners, who respond with anger and attention that serves as a reward for the bird.

Try to determine the schedule of your parrot's screaming. If he usually sounds off at six o'clock in the morning, offer a favorite food or toy before he starts screaming. This may distract him enough to replace his usual performance. But if you're too late and he's already screaming, don't offer anything, or he will learn to scream to *get* a favorite food or toy!

You mustn't pay any attention—positive or negative—to a screaming bird, although you might want to stroll over and cover his cage if you can do it casually and without looking at your bird or talking to him. If he is an eager imitator, try to substitute a more acceptable sound for the screaming. When he sounds off, begin repeating an enthusiastic *beep-beep* or some other inoffensive sound; if he stops screaming to repeat your sound, praise him.

How do you handle feather plucking? This is a distressing syndrome because some birds will strip themselves virtually naked. It's awful to look at a bare chest and stomach, while gorgeous feathers lie spread across the floor.

Your first step is to make an appointment with your vet because feather plucking can have medical causes. Your female bird could have such a powerful nest-building instinct that she is tearing out her own feathers, and your vet may prescribe hormones. If the vet discovers disease, infection, or parasites, he will prescribe antibiotics or sprays. If he discovers that you're feeding a seed-only diet (shame on you!), he will sternly instruct you to include fruits, vegetables, and grains. If he can find no medical or dietary cause for the plucking, it's probably an emotional problem.

That means your bird is feeling stressed, bored, lonely, or anxious. He needs attention. Take him out of his cage more often and talk to him. Give him refreshing baths. Consider a roomier cage, and make sure to place it where it receives plenty of sunlight. Build a new playground or jungle gym. Offer plenty of chew toys and crunchy vegetables to give his restless beak something constructive to do. There are even special collars and jackets that your bird can wear to minimize his ability to pluck.

How do you handle aggression? It may surprise—or embarrass—you to learn that bird aggression is often related to sex. If your bird crouches low on his perch and flutters his wings, he may be trying to "court" you. Yes, indeed, your bird wants to mate with you! You, of course, are horrified by the idea. This makes your bird angry. His anger makes you afraid. Your fear makes him bolder and more likely to bite you.

If you try to appease him by giving him a more suitable mate, things may get worse. Even friendly cockatiels will hiss and attack if you approach the nest, and some don't return to their former sweet selves even after the chicks are gone. You may find that you need to restrict your handling during the breeding season.

Fortunately, most birds are not going to pounce on you and bite without warning. A parrot's warning signs include clicking his beak (often extending his neck and raising one foot at the same time), swiping his beak back and forth against a perch (unless he's just been eating), raising his "hackles" (the feathers on the back of his neck), and spreading his wings while slashing at the air with his open beak.

Be sure you are not misreading a "bite." Parrots use their beaks as a third hand. When they climb onto your hand, they may appear to be biting you when really all they are doing is balancing themselves. Some parrots also nibble affectionately at your collar, hair, ears, and fingers, without any intention of biting. If you react with nervousness, and especially if you jerk away, the bird may become startled and bite defensively.

Biting is a complex problem that requires confident handling. In the classified section of *Bird Talk* magazine you'll find listings of experienced parrot behaviorists who will come to your home and help you work with your bird. Some will even consult with you over the telephone.

Finally, how do you teach your bird to accept petting? Once again, turn to the excellent articles in *Bird Talk*, especially those by Chris Davis and Sally Blanchard.

Often recommended is a peek-a-boo game played with a large soft towel. Take your bird to a different room away from his cage. Maneuver him gently onto a towel spread on the floor. Sit on the floor and play with the corners of the towel, raising and lowering them lightly around the bird with a cheerful "Peek-a-boo!" Most parrots are intrigued with this game and will eventually allow the towel to cover their head. Then you can begin stroking the back of your bird's neck through the towel, and eventually slide your hand under the towel so that your bird is perching on your wrist—through the towel!

This is simply a quick run-through of this fascinating taming technique. It must be done correctly and in a casual, nonthreatening way. Never wrap your bird in the towel and restrain him while you try to pet him.

≈   ≈   ≈

Unfortunately, not all parrots can be tamed to become devoted pets. Sometimes, no matter how hard you try and no matter how much expert advice you obtain, a particular bird simply resists taming. He may be content to share your home with you, but he will refuse your friendship, and you'll find yourself constantly studying his body language just to avoid getting bitten. If you find yourself unhappy with such an aloof bird, consider placing him in a breeding program and looking for a more tamable bird.

10

YOUR BIRD'S CONTINUED GOOD HEALTH

Compared to dogs and cats, birds are strange creatures. Novice owners are always worried about their birds because they don't know much about them. It's hard to know when your bird is doing something abnormal when you don't know what his normal actions should be! So in this chapter we take a closer look at your pet bird and find out what he should and should not be doing in your home.

"Why does my cockatiel keep trying to stick his wings into his water dish?"

He's trying to take a bath. Although birds may not be particularly clean when it comes to their environment (they deposit droppings everywhere, scatter seed, fling fruit, shred newspaper, and whip their toys around), they are exceptionally clean and fussy about their own bodies.

Your bird should preen (groom) himself frequently, running each individual feather through his beak to wipe off the dust and dirt. He may even touch his beak to the base of his tail to get oil from his preening gland. This helps waterproof his feathers and improve their insulating quality. Most birds also love to bathe; in fact, their feathers require moisture for a glowing sheen. Those unfortunate birds who never get to bathe usually have dull and lifeless plumage. For small birds, you can buy a commercial bathhouse that attaches to the outside of his cage door, or you can simply offer a shallow dish such as a clay flowerpot or rubber dog bowl. When filling the dish, remember that birds are not ducks! Put in just enough water to touch his underbelly when he stands up in the dish.

Many birds enjoy a gentle misting from a spray bottle, such as a plant atomizer. They'll spread their wings and flap them all around and open their beaks and squawk happily. Finally, you can offer wet grass or wet lettuce leaves for small birds to roll around on.

"My budgie is shedding his feathers!"

He's molting, which is very similar to shedding. His feathers have simply worn out from time and activity, so they need to fall out and be replaced with new feathers. Molting occurs once or twice a year, (sometimes several times a year), and is seldom a big deal in pet birds. All of your bird's feathers aren't going to fall out at once so that he's naked.

When you start seeing a few feathers here and there, keep checking to be sure the new feathers are growing in with no bald patches. Take extra care that your bird does not get chilled and make sure he is eating pellets and fresh foods and has access to a mineral block and cuttlebone. You'll see "molting conditioning powders" on the pet shop shelves, but don't waste your money.

"Will I have to clip my macaw's toenails like I clip my dog's?"

If you're dreading the idea of cutting your bird's nails, you'll be relieved to hear that natural exercise and climbing usually keep his nails worn down enough.

But if the nails do start curling around into more than a slight curve, head for your bird store. For a couple of dollars, they'll clip the nails quickly and safely and you won't have to deal with a struggling bird. If you decide to clip them yourself, don't cut off so much nail that you cut into the sensitive quick, which is the dark line down the middle of the nail. This will hurt your bird and cause profuse bleeding that must be plugged up quickly. To a small bird, losing even a little precious blood can endanger his life.

"How will I know when to clip my Senegal's wings?"

Since your bird store will probably be doing the clipping, ask them to show you. Wing clipping should always be demonstrated by an expert before you try it—if you ever decide to try it.

Oh, the procedure *sounds* simple enough: you restrain your bird by wrapping him in a soft towel. Then you extend each wing and use sharp scissors to trim the ends off a certain number of flight feathers. If your bird would just sit there placidly, it would be a snap, but most birds put up an outraged struggle, despite the fact their feathers have no feeling in them.

To complicate matters, when a feather is still growing, the shaft of that feather is filled with blood. If you fail to examine each shaft before you cut, you may cut into one of these "blood feathers" and an astounding amount of blood will spurt forth. This is an emergency, and you'll have to grasp the shaft with pliers and pull it out of its socket. This is hard to do with a screaming, struggling bird.

After observing a few clippings, many owners feel confident that they could trim their bird's feathers, but they're content to let the bird store owner be "the bad guy" to their bird!

"My four-year-old Amazon just bobbed his head cheerfully at me and threw up some disgusting stuff!"

Rather than rushing for the phone to call the vet, you should be flattered. Your bird is trying to court you!

What he has done is regurgitate the contents of his crop, a food storage pouch between his mouth and stomach. Sometimes birds do this for no apparent reason. Sometimes they do it to show affection—to demonstrate their willingness to "feed" a prospective mate. If your bird tries to court himself in the mirror, you can remove the mirror, but if he courts you, you'll just have to get used to it!

"When I speak to my pionus parrot or play with him, he fluffs and unfluffs his feathers!"

He's excited! This type of fluffing is usually done with puffs and shakes, and often the bird raises his folded wings so that you can see his "armpits." Many birds will raise their wings and fluff and unfluff themselves whenever you come into the room.

You'll also see fluffing when birds are ready to move from a resting position to a higher level of activity, or when they have groomed themselves. When the temperature is a bit cold, birds may also fluff up to form air pockets between their feathers and create an insulating layer to warm up. These normal behaviors should not be confused with the lethargic, miserable-looking "fluffing up" that birds do when they are sick.

What other normal things might your bird do? He may yawn (if he does this a lot, you should probably open some windows to air out the room). He may stretch one leg backward and, at the same time, extend his wing on the same side; he does this when he's been sitting in one place for a while. He may grind his beak contentedly, especially when he's ready to go to sleep. He may rub his beak against his perch, especially after he has eaten; this cleans the beak and keeps it properly shaped. He may grip his perch and beat his wings up and down as though trying to fly; this is good exercise. He may scratch himself with one foot, which by itself doesn't mean that he has parasites. He may sneeze, especially when he's excited. If the sneeze isn't accompanied by a cough and your bird seems bright and lively, it's perfectly normal.

"Why does my cockatoo have those rough scales on his legs?"

The scales serve as armor to protect the legs. Don't be alarmed by their roughness, but do keep an eye out for swellings, sores, or crusty bumps.

"Why doesn't my finch fall off his perch when he falls asleep?"

His toes automatically lock closed when he falls asleep. Usually birds sleep by turning their head all the way around and nestling their beak into the feathers on their back. They may also *cheep* softly while doing this. Some birds sleep or rest by curling one foot into a tight fist and holding it tucked up into their body; they are feeling very well and contented when they do this. Most birds sleep all night, plus they take frequent short naps during the day.

Some birds seem to enjoy sleeping with their head stuck up inside a clapper bell! Perhaps they think they're hiding: since they can't see anybody, nobody can see them.

"I made a nice playground for my lovebird, but sometimes he flies off it and then I can't catch him!"

Here is where the "Up!" command comes in so handy. You must teach your lovebird to climb onto your extended finger so that when he does fly off and land somewhere, he will wait for you to come "rescue" him. Sometimes a parrot who refuses to climb onto your finger or wrist will consent to climb onto an extended stick.

Until he is responding in this way, you may have to purchase a net to catch him with, or try dropping a towel over him. Making the room as dark as possible also helps, because birds don't see well in the dark and are hesitant to fly. A mischievous bird who keeps flitting around will probably sit tight if you turn out the lights and darken the windows; this gives you a chance to sneak up and catch him.

"My canary is usually tame, but when I hold him gently in my hand, his heart goes lickety-split!"

First of all, very few canaries appreciate being handled. More important, any bird will panic if you put your hand around his chest! We have a diaphragm that moves air in and out of our lungs, so we can breathe without having to expand our chest. Birds have no diaphragm; their lungs expand only when their entire chest expands. If you wrap your fingers around your bird's chest so that it cannot fully expand, he will suffocate— so naturally his heart is going lickety-split! A bird's heart rate is extremely fast, anyway. Our heart beats 70 to 80 times a minute, while the heart of a macaw beats about 200 times a minute, and the heart of a canary beats about 600 times a minute.

"We want to paint our family room. Will painting fumes harm my Pekin robins?"

Yes. Birds are extremely sensitive to all types of fumes. You should move the cage to another room and leave it there for at least a week after the painting has been completed. In the same way, if you find a trail of ants crawling across your floor and feel obliged to break out the Raid, move your birds into another room first. Then open the doors and windows and air the room out thoroughly before allowing the birds to return. If you are a smoker, please don't do it around your birds.

"Why does my sun conure 'tongue' all his foods and toys to death?"

Unlike your dog and cat, your bird doesn't have a good sense of smell. He does, however, compensate with an excellent sense of taste. His tongue may look thick and clunky, but it's extremely delicate and can be manipulated with ease. He will use his tongue to sift through an entire seed cup, gobbling the seeds he likes and dramatically spitting out the ones he doesn't like. He will also "explore" his toys and playthings—and your fingers—with his tongue.

"Help! My Quaker parakeet has no ears!"

Actually, he just has no ear lobes. His ears are simply ear canals leading down into his head. If you part his feathers just below and behind his eyes, you'll be able to see the holes. One of the reasons your bird can fly is that he is built so lightly and efficiently. Ear lobes are not essential, so they've been eliminated. Ear lobes would also allow heat loss, and it's important that birds conserve heat to maintain their high body temperature.

Your bird is built efficiently in other ways, too. He has no teeth, no tonsils, no diaphragm, and no urinary bladder. All of these would be too heavy to tote around. Many of his bones are hollow and filled with air. We do share some unfortunate health problems with birds, though. Like humans, birds are susceptible to strokes, heart attacks, diabetes, and cancer.

"My caique insists on nibbling at my plants! How do I know which ones are poisonous?"

If your caique persists in flying or climbing off his playground, you need to persist in placing him back on it with a firm "Up!" command. If he leaves more than twice, put him back in his cage. He will soon learn that being on the playground is a privilege that you will revoke if taken advantage of. He also needs more supervision so that he doesn't have the chance to get to your plants.

Some common plants that are potentially dangerous to birds include amaryllis, azalea, boxwood, buckthorn, buttercup, caladium, castor bean, Christmas cherry, clematis, coral plant, cowslip, daffodil, dieffenbachia, English holly, hemlock, hyacinth, hydrangea, iris, ivy, jimsonweed, lantana, larkspur, lily of the valley, mistletoe, morning glory, narcissus, nightshade, nutmeg, oleander, philodendron, rhododendron, rhubarb, and yew.

***"My budgie goes to the bathroom every half-hour or so, and his droppings
are . . . um . . . sort of funny-looking!"***

Birds have a very high metabolism. Food must go in and out of their body
frequently so that they always have fresh fuel for quick flight. Since too much
food in the body would slow down flying, they eliminate unused material 25
to 50 times a day. For further efficiency, they only have a single opening for
waste, so solid and liquid wastes are combined. The firm bottom part (feces)
is black or green, while the soft top part (urine) is white. A few droppings
each day may be shapeless and watery, but that's not a problem so long as
most of the droppings are normal. Fruit-eating birds such as lories and mynahs
have very loose droppings all the time.

"How can I tell if my African grey is sick?"

The same checklist you used to examine your bird before you purchased him
(pages 155–156) should be used daily in your home. But no list of symptoms
can substitute for knowing your own bird. When your bird doesn't look the
way he usually does and when he isn't acting the way he usually does, your
antennae should go up, just as they do when your kids don't seem "right."
That means observing your bird and spending time with your bird when he is
healthy, so that you can quickly spot the difference.

Daily observation and quick spotting of changes are important because
birds hide symptoms for as long as they can. Their stoicism is a survival tactic;
wild birds are quick to attack a sick or weak individual. But in your home
it means that when you do notice a symptom, the illness may already be quite
advanced. Whenever your bird stops eating or looks or acts differently, call
your vet and follow instructions. Bird illnesses seldom go away on their own,
and you will have no success treating them with the generic "medicines"
you'll find at pet shops.

"What are the most common illnesses of birds?"

Colds and intestinal disorders. With colds, you'll see coughing (little clicks),
sneezing (very tiny), wheezing, nasal discharge, and an apathetic look.
Intestinal disorders are usually recognized by apathy and shapeless watery
droppings. Any time your bird stops eating, you've got a problem because the
high metabolism and high body temperature of birds require frequent meals.

The first thing to do is to call your vet, who may tell you to set up a hospital cage. A hospital cage means quiet and warm. Move your bird's cage to a back bedroom. Cover the cage with a towel. Slide a heating pad under the cage, or place an infrared heat lamp so that the front half of the cage is between 85 and 90 degrees, while the back half is a normal 70 degrees. Use a thermometer to check temperatures; you don't want to fry your bird. But don't place the thermometer where the bird can get to it! Remove all toys, and all perches except the lowest one. Place food and water dishes on the floor in the back. Along with his usual foods, offer camomile tea, cooked rice, and hard-boiled egg. If there is no improvement in two days, call the vet again.

"Can my mynah bird get doggy illnesses, such as fleas or distemper?"

Most people know that dogs and cats are prone to fleas and ticks. Birds usually are not, but they are susceptible to mites and lice. Indoor birds that you've had for a while are unlikely to develop these parasites, but you might see them in new birds, imported birds, or outdoor aviary birds. Nonetheless, all birds should be checked periodically for scaly white deposits at the corners of their beak and on their legs and toes. Also check for tiny red or white moving specks on the feathers or perches. Watch for excessive scratching and a moth-eaten appearance. Your vet will prescribe an ointment or insecticide, and a more frequent cage-cleaning routine.

Your bird could also develop worms, as well as a microscopic protozoan called giardia. These can be detected only by bringing a sample of your bird's droppings to your vet for a simple laboratory analysis. You might suspect them if your bird is doing poorly.

You may have heard of distemper in dogs and leukemia in cats, but birds have their own group of "big" diseases. Psittacosis, also called ornithosis or chlamydiosis, is caused by very tough bacteria. Some birds carry this dreaded disease for years without showing symptoms, but eventually they start to do poorly, and exhibit loose green droppings and/or odd head tremors. The other big disease is psittacine beak and feather syndrome, which is most commonly seen in cockatoos. The feathers fall out and are replaced with curled or deformed ones, while the beak changes color and shape. Your bird's immune system is affected, so he becomes susceptible to secondary infections.

"Can I catch any illnesses from my bird? Might I be allergic to birds?"

Infectious diseases that can pass from bird to human include psittacosis and giardiosis. If you suffer serious cold, flu, or digestive symptoms that just won't go away, tell your doctor that you keep birds.

If you have allergies, you may have a problem with birds. Indeed, some statistics suggest that more people are allergic to birds than to cats! Although the powdery feathers on cockatoos and cockatiels are a special problem, it is not so much the feathers of birds as the dust that birds create. Bird droppings quickly dry out and turn to dust, which then is in the air of your house.

Allergic owners who are determined to keep birds moisten the newspapers on the bottom of the cage so that the dust does not fly up so much. They also change the papers two or three times a day. Seed cups should be changed just as frequently so that empty seed hulls don't end up flying around. An air purifier in the bird's room is an excellent idea.

"If my ringnecked parakeet gets hurt, can I use the supplies in our family first aid kit?"

Ideally, your bird should have his own first aid kit stored within easy reach of his cage. Include a small bottle of Kwik-Stop powder and cotton to stop bleeding from your bird's beak or nails. Include a thick absorbent cloth to stop bleeding elsewhere. Include a Co-Flex cohesive bandage to immobilize injured areas long enough to get the bird to the vet. Finally, include a pair of pliers or forceps to pull out broken blood feathers.

Also pack a food emergency kit (pellets and seeds) for that inevitable time when you run out of food on Christmas Eve. Keep replacing the food so that it never gets old or stale. If you live where earthquakes, hurricanes, blizzards, or floods are common (I think that covers most of the United States!), you'll be glad to have these rations should you be cut off from "civilization" for a few days.

"How do I choose a good vet?"

The first rule is to find an avian vet before you need one. Ten o'clock on a Friday night is not the time to riffle through the phone book making frantic calls. "Hello, do you treat birds?" "Sorry to call so late, but do you treat birds?" "Yes, hello, do you treat birds? You do? Listen, I have a Moluccan lory who . . . pardon me? A lory is a type of parrot! I thought you said you treated birds!"

Finding a good avian vet can be difficult. The number of pet birds is rapidly approaching the number of pet dogs and cats, but birds are not seen by veterinarians very much, so most vets are not experienced at diagnosing, treating, or even handling birds. Some vets will honestly admit that they're a little afraid of birds.

When searching for a vet, bypass the ones who list birds along with dogs, cats, rabbits, and rodents. You want someone who *specializes* in birds. Check your Yellow Pages under *Veterinarians*. If the Yellow Pages lists a veterinary referral service, call them first. Also call bird stores and breeders and ask them for veterinary recommendations. When you do find a potential vet, ask for a tour of the facilities; they're accustomed to this and won't mind at all. If the vet doesn't have an incubator, heat lamps, and special bird syringes and feeding tubes, he isn't the vet for you.

As you can see, it can be difficult to detect and treat bird illnesses, so prevention is extremely important. Once you understand that many health problems are brought on by stress, you can work hard to prevent stress. Provide a roomy cage, plenty of light and sunshine, a varied diet, interesting toys, free playtime, a reasonably predictable schedule, and plenty of companionship.

Avoid too much change. The harmless little changes that your bird might consider stressful could literally fill the pages of a book: a new noise (your gurgling fish filter), a new food (green apple rather than red), a new toy (six beads instead of four), a new tile floor, a house guest, a new baby, a new pet.

Chewbacca, a Moluccan cockatoo accustomed to his owner strolling in the front door at 6:15, stared in shock when the owner came home sick one day. When the owner approached his cage he shrieked, scrambled up the bars, and refused to eat that evening's dinner. This is not atypical of parrots. It bears repeating: birds can be made ill by stress, and stress can be caused by too much change.

APPENDIX
BIRD SOURCES AND
CONTACTS

Acadiana Aviaries; 2500 Chatsworth Road; Franklin, LA 70538

African Lovebird Society; Box 142; San Marcos, CA 92069

American Cage-Bird magazine; One Glamore Court; Smithtown, NY 11787 (516) 979-7962

American Cockatiel Society; Box 111; Marlin, TX 76661

American Singers Club; Jessie Durkin; 3564 Loon Lake Road; Wixom, MI 48393 (Canaries)

Bird & Board; Shelli and Michael Pollin; 292 South Tustin; Orange, CA 92666

Bird Talk magazine; Box 6050; Mission Viejo, CA 92690 (714) 855-8822

Cockatiel Connection; Dawn Miller; 207 Banks Station #700; Fayetteville, GA 30214

Charles Collins; 901 South First Street; LaPorte, TX 77571 (Indian Ringnecks)

Diana Holloway; 235 North Walnut Street; Bryan, OH 43506 (Amazons, Dwarf Macaws)

House of Earl; 1509 North El Camino Real; San Clemente, CA 92672

Loridae Production Network; Box 575; Woodlake, CA 93286 (Lories and Lorikeets)

Carolyn Mauro; Parrots of the Rainforest; Windham, NH; State Representative of the Macaw Society of America

Mynah News; Linda Leger; 641 Invader; Sulphur, LA 70663

Omar's Exotic Birds; 25401 Alicia Parkway; Laguna Hills, CA 92653

Daunice Parker; Southern Charmers; Box 1677; Metairie, LA 70001 (Amazons, African greys, Senegals)

The Rabrens; K.D.'s Exotic Birds; 8051 Valmoral Drive; Mobile, AL 36619 (Quakers)

Twin Willows Aviaries; Box 547; Byron, CA 94514

INDEX

(Page numbers in **boldface** refer to species profiles.
Page numbers in *italic* refer to illustrations.)

PHOTO CREDITS

Grateful acknowledgment is made for permission to use the following photographs (in order of appearance):

Peach-faced Lovebirds (title page): Lee Horton

Eclectus (page 1): B. Everett Webb/Nature's Moments Photography

Red-cheeked Cordon Bleus (page 21): B. Everett Webb/Nature's Moments Photography

Perched grouping of species—Greater Sulphur-crested Cockatoo; Yellow-naped Amazon; Yellow-collared Macaw; Lutino Peach-faced Lovebird; Sun Conure; Lutino Cockatiel; African Grey (page 45): B. Everett Webb/Nature's Moments Photography

African Grey (Congo) (page 47): Omar's Exotic Birds

African Grey (Timneh) (page 50): Scott Swickard

Yellow-crowned Amazons (page 51): Diana Holloway